ENTERTAIN with EASE

A dinner party is a wonderful way to entertain, but gone are the days when you would spend days preparing the meal. Entertain with Ease presents complete menus for twelve easy dinner parties. This book takes the hard work out of having a dinner party – the menus have been worked out for you and the dishes are easy yet stylish.

CONTENTS

THE PANTRY SHELF

Unless otherwise stated the following ingredients used in this book are:

Cream	Double, suitable for whipping
Flour	White flour, plain or standard
Sugar	White sugar

WHAT'S IN A TABLESPOON

AUSTRALIA
1 tablespoon =
20 mL or 4 teaspoons
NEW ZEALAND
1 tablespoon =
15 mL or 3 teaspoons
UNITED KINGDOM
1 tablespoon =
15 mL or 3 teaspoons
The recipes in this book were tested in Australia where a 20 mL tablespoon is standard. All measures are level. The tablespoon in the New Zealand and United Kingdom sets of measuring spoons is 15 mL. For recipes using baking powder, gelatine, bicarbonate of soda, small quantities of flour and cornflour, simply add another teaspoon for each tablespoon specified.

Very Special Occasion

Baby Spinach Tarts

Tuna with Wasabi Butter

Grilled Vegetable Stacks

Lamb on Pastry Diamonds

Sweet Potato Timbales

Gingered Baby Beets

Fresh Mint Chutney

Chocolate Decadence

SERVES 10

Baby Spinach Tarts

Oven temperature
200°C, 400°F, Gas 6

The pastry cases can be made up to 3 days in advance and stored in an airtight container. Or make the cases several weeks in advance and freeze them. The filling mixture can be made earlier in the day, then covered and kept in the refrigerator until just prior to cooking.

PASTRY
1^1/2 cups/185 g/6 oz flour
4 tablespoons grated Parmesan cheese
100 g/3^1/2 oz butter, chopped
2-3 tablespoons iced water

SPINACH FILLING
2 teaspoons olive oil
2 spring onions, chopped
1 clove garlic, crushed
8 spinach leaves, shredded
125 g/4 oz ricotta cheese, drained
2 eggs, lightly beaten
^{1}/3 cup/90 mL/3 fl oz milk
^{1}/2 teaspoon grated nutmeg
4 tablespoons pine nuts

1   To make pastry, place flour, Parmesan cheese and butter in a food processor and process until mixture resembles fine breadcrumbs.

2   With machine running, slowly add enough water to form a soft dough. Turn dough onto a lightly floured surface and knead briefly. Wrap dough in plastic food wrap and refrigerate for 30 minutes.

3   Roll out pastry to 3 mm/^{1}/8 in thick. Using an 8 cm/3^1/2 in fluted pastry cutter, cut out twenty pastry rounds. Place pastry rounds in lightly greased patty tins. Pierce base and sides of pastry with a fork and bake for 5-10 minutes or until lightly golden.

4   To make filling, heat oil in a frying pan over a medium heat. Add spring onions, garlic and spinach and cook, stirring, until spinach is wilted. Remove pan from heat and set aside to cool.

5   Place spinach mixture, ricotta cheese, eggs, milk and nutmeg in a bowl and mix to combine. Spoon filling into pastry cases and sprinkle with pine nuts. Reduce oven temperature to 180°C/350°F/Gas 4 and bake for 15-20 minutes or until tarts are golden and filling is set.

Makes 20

Tuna with Wasabi Butter

If fresh tuna is unavailable use fresh salmon fillet instead. It is important that you use absolutely fresh fish for this recipe. Prepare about 1 hour prior to serving. The Wasabi Butter can be made several days in advance and stored in an airtight container in the refrigerator. Allow it to come to room temperature, then beat it again before using.

250 g/8 oz tuna steaks, cut
1 cm/^{1}/2 in thick
20 small rounds pumpernickel bread

GINGER MARINADE
2 teaspoons sesame oil
1 tablespoon soy sauce
1 clove garlic, crushed
2 teaspoons grated fresh ginger

WASABI BUTTER
75 g/2^1/2 oz butter, softened
^{1}/2-1 teaspoon wasabi paste or wasabi powder mixed with water to form a paste
2 tablespoons chopped fresh coriander

1   To make marinade, place oil, soy sauce, garlic and ginger in a bowl and mix to combine. Cut tuna into thin slices. Add to marinade and toss to coat. Cover and set aside to marinate for 1 hour. Drain.

2   To make Wasabi Butter, place butter, wasabi paste and coriander in a small bowl and beat until smooth.

3   Spread pumpernickel rounds with Wasabi Butter, then top with tuna slices. Cover and chill until ready to serve.

Makes 20

Sweet Potato Timbales

1.5 kg/3 lb orange sweet potatoes,
roughly chopped
2 leeks, cut in half lengthwise,
leaves separated
2 teaspoons ground cumin
3 tablespoons chopped fresh coriander
3 eggs, lightly beaten
1 cup/250 mL/8 fl oz cream (double)

1 Cook sweet potatoes in boiling water for 10 minutes or until tender. Drain well and set aside to cool slightly.

2 Blanch leeks in boiling water for 1 minute or until soft. Drain and set aside.

Tuna with Wasabi Butter, Baby Spinach Tarts

3 Place sweet potatoes in a blender or food processor and process until smooth. Transfer purée to a bowl. Add cumin, coriander, eggs and cream and mix to combine.

4 Line ten oiled timbale moulds with leek leaves, leaving some of the leaves to hang over the side. Divide sweet potato mixture evenly between moulds and fold leek leaves over the top.

5 Place moulds in a baking dish with enough boiling water to come halfway up the sides of the moulds and bake for 25-30 minutes or until firm. To serve, invert moulds and tap base of mould to release.

Makes 10

Oven temperature
160°C, 325°F, Gas 3

This recipe can be made ahead of time up to the end of step 4. Cover and refrigerate the timbales until you are ready to bake them. If you do not have timbale moulds use small ramekins instead.

LAMB ON PASTRY DIAMONDS

Oven temperature
200°C, 400°F, Gas 6

5 x 375 g/12 oz lamb fillets or 2 kg/4 lb
lamb back straps, trimmed of all
visible fat and sinew
1 tablespoon vegetable oil
15 g/^{1}/$_2$ oz butter
500 g/1 lb prepared puff pastry
1 egg, lightly beaten

RED WINE MARINADE
300 mL/9^1/$_2$ fl oz red wine
2 cloves garlic, crushed
2 teaspoons crushed black peppercorns
2 tablespoons honey

1   Cut each fillet in half or cut lamb back straps to give ten pieces.

2   To make marinade, place wine, garlic, black pepper and honey in a large bowl and mix to combine. Add lamb and toss to coat. Set aside to marinate for 2 hours.

3   Drain lamb and pat dry with absorbent kitchen paper. Heat oil and butter together in a large frying pan over a medium heat, until sizzling. Add lamb and cook, turning until browned on all sides. Transfer lamb to a baking dish and bake for 15-20 minutes or until cooked to your liking.

4   Roll out pastry to 5 mm/^{1}/$_4$ in thick and cut into ten 12 cm/5^3/$_4$ in long diamond shapes. Place pastry diamonds on a greased baking tray, brush with egg and bake for 10 minutes or until puffed and golden.

5   To serve, slice lamb and arrange on pastry diamonds. Accompany with Fresh Mint Chutney.

Serves 10

GINGERED BABY BEETS

The cooking time for the beetroot will vary depending on their size. Very small beetroot were used for this recipe. If these are unavailable use larger ones but remember to increase the cooking time.

1^1/$_2$ cups/375 mL/12 fl oz chicken stock
2 tablespoons grated fresh ginger
5 cardamom pods
10 uncooked baby beetroot, peeled,
with stems left intact

1   Place chicken stock in a large saucepan and bring to the boil over a medium heat. Add ginger and cardamom and boil for 2 minutes.

2   Reduce heat to simmering, add beetroot and simmer for 7-10 minutes or until tender. Drain. Serve warm.

Serves 10

Grilled Vegetable Stacks

GRILLED VEGETABLE STACKS

300 g/9¹/2 oz firm goat's cheese,
cut into 10 slices
¹/4 cup/60 mL/2 fl oz olive oil
2 cloves garlic, crushed
2 teaspoons crushed black peppercorns
3 yellow or green peppers,
cut into large pieces
3 red peppers, cut into large pieces
4 zucchini (courgettes), cut into
long thin strips
2 eggplant (aubergines), thinly sliced
20 radicchio leaves
1 bunch/250 g/8 oz watercress,
broken into sprigs

THYME DRESSING
¹/2 cup/125 mL/4 fl oz balsamic
or red wine vinegar
2 tablespoons fresh thyme leaves
or 1 teaspoon dried thyme
¹/4 cup/60 mL/2 fl oz orange juice

Serves 10

1 Place goat's cheese slices on a baking
tray and cook under a preheated hot grill
for 1-2 minutes or until just golden.

2 Place oil, garlic and black pepper in a
bowl and whisk to combine. Brush yellow
or green peppers, red peppers, zucchini
(courgettes), eggplant (aubergines) and
radicchio with oil mixture and cook under
a preheated hot grill for 2 minutes each
side or until vegetables are tender.

3 To make dressing, place vinegar,
thyme and orange juice in a bowl and
whisk to combine.

4 To assemble, place layers of alternating
vegetables on individual serving plates.
Place a few sprigs of watercress between
each layer of vegetables. Sprinkle with
dressing and top with a slice of goat's
cheese. Cover and refrigerate until ready
to serve.

This recipe is best made
several hours in advance, as
the flavours develop on
standing.

FRESH MINT CHUTNEY

This chutney is best made on the day of serving. If kept for too long it tends to lose its colour.

Chocolate Decadence

1 large bunch fresh mint, leaves removed and finely chopped
2 tablespoons lemon juice
125 g/4 oz pine nuts, toasted
2 tablespoons honey
2 teaspoons crushed black peppercorns

Place mint, lemon juice, pine nuts, honey and black pepper in a bowl and mix well to combine. Store in an airtight container in the refrigerator.

Makes 1^1/$_2$ cups/375 g/12 oz

CHOCOLATE DECADENCE

CHOCOLATE CAKE
1 cup/100 g/3¹/2 oz cocoa powder
1¹/2 cups/375 mL/12 fl oz boiling water
375 g/12 oz butter, softened
1 teaspoon vanilla essence
1¹/2 cups/330 g/10¹/2 oz caster sugar
4 eggs
2¹/2 cups/315 g/10 oz flour
¹/2 cup/60 g/2 oz cornflour
1 teaspoon bicarbonate of soda

CHOCOLATE CREAM
90 g/3 oz milk chocolate, melted
1 tablespoon brandy
¹/2 cup/125 mL/4 fl oz cream (double),
whipped

MOULDING CHOCOLATE
200 g/6¹/2 oz chocolate (milk,
dark or white)
75 mL/2¹/2 fl oz liquid glucose

1 To make cake, place cocoa powder and water in a bowl and mix to make a smooth paste. Set aside to cool.

2 Place butter, vanilla essence and sugar in a bowl and beat until light and creamy. Beat in eggs one at a time, beating well after each addition.

3 Sift together flour, cornflour and bicarbonate of soda. Fold flour mixture and cocoa mixture, alternately, into egg mixture.

4 Spoon batter into two greased and lined 25 cm/10 in round cake tins and bake for 30-35 minutes or until cooked when tested with a skewer. Stand in tins for 5 minutes before turning onto wire racks to cool.

5 To make Chocolate Cream, fold melted chocolate and brandy into cream. Spread over top of one cake then top with remaining cake.

5 To make Moulding Chocolate, place chocolate in a heatproof bowl set over a saucepan of simmering water and heat, stirring, until chocolate melts. Remove bowl from heat, set aside and allow chocolate to cool to lukewarm. Stir in glucose and mix until the chocolate leaves the sides of the bowl and forms a ball. Take care not to overmix or chocolate will separate. You should stop stirring as soon as the mixture is combined.

7 Wrap Moulding Chocolate in plastic food wrap and refrigerate for 30 minutes or until firm. Remove Moulding Chocolate from the refrigerator and knead in your hands until pliable.

8 Take tablespoons of Moulding Chocolate and roll into flat irregular shapes. Drape over cake.

Makes a 25 cm/10 in round cake

Oven temperature
180°C, 350°F, Gas 4

The Chocolate Cake can be made the day before and stored in an airtight container. Or make a week in advance and freeze it. The Moulding Chocolate can be made 1-2 days in advance and stored in the refrigerator.
The final assembly of the dessert can be done up to 6 hours in advance. Store in the refrigerator until ready to serve.

Italian Connection

Innovative Antipasto Platter

*Pasta with Roasted Garlic
and Tomatoes*

Veal with Lemon Basil Sauce

Eggplant Purée

*Steamed Vegetables or Salad
(optional)*

Nougat Tartufo

SERVES 8

Vegetable and Herb Crisps

3 zucchini (courgettes)
1 large eggplant (aubergine),
thinly sliced
salt
vegetable oil for deep-frying
20 fresh basil leaves
20 fresh sage leaves
20 small sprigs flat-leaved parsley

1   Using a vegetable peeler, peel long thin strips from zucchini (courgettes). Place zucchini (courgettes) and eggplant (aubergine) in a colander, sprinkle with salt and set aside to stand for 20 minutes.

2   Rinse vegetables under cold running water and pat dry with absorbent kitchen paper.

3   Heat oil in a large saucepan until a cube of bread dropped in browns in 50 seconds. Cook vegetables and herbs in batches for 2-3 minutes or until crisp. Remove, using a slotted spoon, drain on absorbent kitchen paper and serve immediately with Three-Cheese Dip.

Serves 8

The antipasto platter uses a combination of purchased and homemade foods. Purchase the olives, sun-dried peppers, cheese and bread. If time is short you may prefer to purchase everything for the platter. You could include sun-dried tomatoes and marinated artichoke hearts – see what your delicatessen has to offer.

Crunchy Prosciutto

12 slices prosciutto
2 tablespoons balsamic or
red wine vinegar
2 cloves garlic, crushed

1   Cut prosciutto slices in half, lengthwise. Place vinegar and garlic in a small bowl and whisk to combine .

2   Brush prosciutto with vinegar mixture and cook under a preheated medium grill for 1-2 minutes each side or until crisp. Serve warm or cold.

Serves 8

To serve the antipasto platter, attractively arrange Vegetable and Herb Crisps, Three-Cheese Dip and Crunchy Prosciutto with olives, peppers, cheese and bread on a large platter. The antipasto can be handed around with drinks as finger food, or you might like to place the platter in the middle of the table so that your guests can sit around the table and help themselves.

Innovative Antipasto Platter

THREE-CHEESE DIP

125 g/4 oz creamy blue cheese,
crumbled
125 g/4 oz ricotta cheese, drained
125 g/4 oz provolone cheese, grated
1 tablespoon sour cream
3 tablespoons snipped fresh chives
1 tablespoon lemon juice
1 teaspoon crushed black peppercorns

1   Place blue cheese, ricotta cheese,
provolone cheese and sour cream in a
bowl and mix well to combine.

2   Stir in chives, lemon juice and black
pepper. Cover and chill until required.

Serves 8

This dip can be made 2-3
days in advance and stored
in a covered container in the
refrigerator.

PASTA WITH ROASTED GARLIC AND TOMATOES

When garlic is roasted it loses its pungent strong taste and odour and becomes sweet and subtle.
If plum (egg or Italian) tomatoes are unavailable, this recipe can be made using small ordinary tomatoes.

2 tablespoons olive oil
16 plum (egg or Italian) tomatoes, quartered
32 cloves garlic, unpeeled
sea salt
500 g/1 lb fresh fettuccine

MINT PESTO
1 large bunch fresh mint
4 tablespoons grated Parmesan cheese
1 clove garlic, crushed
3 tablespoons pine nuts
3 tablespoons olive oil

1   Place oil, tomatoes and garlic in a large baking dish. Toss to coat and sprinkle with sea salt. Bake for 35 minutes or until garlic is deep brown in colour. Keep warm.

2   To make pesto, place mint leaves, Parmesan cheese, garlic and pine nuts in a food processor or blender and process until finely chopped. With machine running, gradually add oil and continue processing until a thick paste forms.

3   Cook pasta in boiling water in a large saucepan following packet directions. Drain and keep warm.

4   Just prior to serving, remove skin from garlic cloves. To serve, divide hot pasta between serving plates, then top with some of the roasted tomatoes and roasted garlic and a spoonful of Mint Pesto.

Serves 8

EGGPLANT PUREE

750 g/1¹/₂ lb eggplant (aubergines),
peeled and chopped
2 cloves garlic, crushed
³/₄ cup/185 mL/6 fl oz cream (double)
100 g/3¹/₂ oz butter

1   Boil or microwave eggplant
(aubergines) until very tender. Drain well
and set aside to cool slightly.

2   Place eggplant (aubergines), garlic and
cream in a food processor or blender and
process until smooth. Place purée in a
small saucepan and heat over a low heat,
stirring, for 3-4 minutes or until hot.

3   Place butter in a small saucepan and
cook over a low heat until brown. To
serve, drizzle browned butter over
spoonfuls of purée.

Left: Pasta with Roasted Garlic and Tomatoes
Above: Eggplant Purée, Veal with Lemon Basil
Sauce (page 16)

Serves 8

The purée can be made in
advance and reheated just
prior to serving. It will reheat
well in the microwave.

VEAL WITH LEMON BASIL SAUCE

This recipe is also delicious
made using turkey schnitzels
(escalopes) instead of veal.

8 veal schnitzels (escalopes)
1 tablespoon olive oil

RICOTTA AND TOMATO FILLING
250 g/8 oz ricotta cheese, drained
10 sun-dried tomatoes, chopped
125 g/4 oz pitted black olives, chopped
4 canned artichoke hearts, drained
and finely chopped
1 tablespoon green peppercorns
in brine, drained

LEMON BASIL SAUCE
$^1/_2$ bunch fresh basil, leaves removed
and shredded
1 cup/250 mL/8 fl oz cream (double)
6 strips lemon rind

1   To make filling, place ricotta cheese,
sun-dried tomatoes, olives, artichokes
and green peppercorns in a bowl and
mix to combine.

2   Place spoonfuls of filling down the
centre of each veal schnitzel (escalope).
Fold in sides, roll up veal and secure with
toothpicks.

3   Heat oil in a large frying pan. Add
veal rolls and cook, turning occasionally,
for 3-5 minutes or until golden and
cooked. Remove from pan and keep
warm.

4   To make sauce, place basil, cream and
lemon rind in a saucepan and cook over a
low heat, stirring, for 3 minutes. Remove
lemon rind.

5   To serve, slice veal rolls into
medallions and serve with sauce.

Serves 8

You may also like to serve
steamed green vegetables,
such as asparagus or green
beans, or a tossed salad of
mixed lettuces with the main
course of this meal.

NOUGAT TARTUFO

200 g/6$^1/_2$ oz nougat, chopped
60 g/2 oz hazelnuts, toasted and chopped
60 g/2 oz slivered almonds, toasted
200 g/6$^1/_2$ oz dark or milk
chocolate, chopped
2 litres/3$^1/_2$ pt vanilla ice cream,
softened
3 tablespoons honey
$^1/_2$ cup/45 g/1$^1/_2$ oz shredded
coconut, toasted

1   Place nougat, hazelnuts, almonds,
chocolate, ice cream and honey in a bowl
and mix carefully to combine.

2   Spoon ice cream mixture into eight
1 cup/250 mL/8 fl oz capacity chilled
aluminium moulds lined with plastic food
wrap and freeze for 1 hour.

3   Remove moulds from freezer and
unmould. Roll ice cream in coconut.
Place on a tray lined with plastic food
wrap, cover and freeze until required.

Serves 8

To toast nuts, place them in a
single layer on a baking tray
or in a shallow ovenproof
dish and bake at 180°C/
350°F/Gas 4 for 10-15 minutes
or until they are golden. Turn
them several times during
cooking. Set aside to cool.

Seafood Sampler

Marinated Baby Octopus

Oysters with Gravlax

Scallops with Mango Salsa

Salmon on Zucchini Flans

Warm Seafood Salad

Scampi with Basil Butter

Miniature Passion Fruit Bavarois

SERVES 8

MARINATED BABY OCTOPUS

1 kg/2 lb baby octopus, cleaned

SPICY MARINADE
2 cloves garlic, crushed
2 tablespoons grated fresh ginger
2 fresh red chillies, finely chopped
3 tablespoons lime juice
2 teaspoons finely grated lime rind
3 tablespoons balsamic or
red wine vinegar
1 tablespoon olive oil
3 tablespoons chopped fresh coriander

To clean octopus, remove heads by cutting just below the eyes. Remove beaks and wash octopus well. Fresh octopus will keep in the refrigerator for up to 2 days. Clean it before storing and store in plastic food wrap. Octopus can also be frozen for up to 3 months.

1   To make marinade, place garlic, ginger, chillies, lime juice, lime rind, vinegar, oil and coriander in a large bowl and whisk to combine.

2   Add octopus and toss to coat. Cover and refrigerate overnight.

3   Drain octopus and cook under a preheated hot grill for 4-5 minutes or until tender.

Serves 8

SCALLOPS WITH MANGO SALSA

16 scallops in half shells
freshly ground black pepper

MANGO SALSA
1 mango, peeled and chopped
1 tablespoon chopped fresh mint
1 tablespoon lemon juice
2 tablespoons sesame seeds, toasted

If fresh mango is unavailable, drained canned mango can be used instead for the salsa. The salsa can be made earlier in the day and stored, covered, in the refrigerator until required.
If you wish to serve this dish chilled, cook the scallops 2-3 hours in advance and chill until ready to serve.

1   To make salsa, place mango, mint, lemon juice and sesame seeds in a small bowl and mix to combine. Cover and refrigerate until required.

2   Bring a large saucepan of water to the boil. Add scallops and cook for 1 minute or until tender. Using a slotted spoon remove scallops from water and place on a serving platter. Serve warm or chilled, seasoned with black pepper and topped with salsa.

Serves 8

Oysters with Gravlax, Scallops with Mango Salsa, Marinated Baby Octopus

OYSTERS WITH GRAVLAX

250 g/8 oz gravlax or smoked
salmon slices
16 oysters in the shell
3 tablespoons lemon juice
freshly ground black pepper

1   Cut gravlax or smoked salmon into
long strips. Loosen oysters in shells.

2   Top oysters with gravlax or smoked
salmon slices. Sprinkle with lemon juice
and season with black pepper. Cover and
refrigerate until required.

Serves 8

This recipe can be prepared
earlier in the day and kept
chilled until required.

Plates Limoges Australia

SCAMPI WITH BASIL BUTTER

8 uncooked scampi or yabbies,
heads removed

BASIL BUTTER
90 g/3 oz butter, melted
2 tablespoons chopped fresh basil
1 clove garlic, crushed
2 teaspoons honey

Serves 8

1   Cut scampi or yabbies in half,
lengthwise.

2   To make Basil Butter, place butter,
basil, garlic and honey in a small bowl
and whisk to combine.

3   Brush cut side of each scampi or
yabbie half with Basil Butter and cook
under a preheated hot grill for 2 minutes
or until they change colour and are
tender. Drizzle with any remaining Basil
Butter and serve immediately.

SALMON ON ZUCCHINI FLANS

Oven temperature
180°C, 350°F, Gas 4

2 x 500 g/1 lb salmon fillets
2 tablespoons olive oil
2 tablespoons lime juice
2 teaspoons crushed black peppercorns

ZUCCHINI (COURGETTE) FLANS
4 green zucchini (courgettes)
4 yellow zucchini (courgettes)
4 tablespoons grated Parmesan cheese
4 tablespoons grated tasty cheese
(mature Cheddar)

Using two different-coloured
zucchini (courgettes) makes
a very attractive dish, but
you can make this recipe
using just green zucchini
(courgettes). It still looks
wonderful and is just as
delicious.

Serves 8

1   Cut each salmon fillet into four pieces.
Combine oil, lime juice and black pepper.
Brush salmon with oil mixture. Cook
salmon under a preheated hot grill or in a
preheated grill pan for 2 minutes each
side or until flesh flakes when tested with
a fork. Keep warm.

2   To make flans, cut green and yellow
zucchini (courgettes) diagonally into thin
slices. Cook zucchini (courgette) slices in
boiling water for 1 minute, then drain
well. Arrange green and yellow zucchini
(courgette) slices, alternately and
overlapping them slightly, to form eight
circles on greased baking trays.

3   Combine Parmesan cheese and tasty
cheese (mature Cheddar) and sprinkle
over flans. Bake for 12 minutes or until
cheese is melted and golden.

4   Using a spatula, carefully lift flans
from baking tray and place on a serving
platter. Place a piece of salmon across the
top of each flan and serve immediately.

*Warm Seafood Salad (page 22), Scampi with
Basil Butter, Salmon on Zucchini Flans*

Warm Seafood Salad

500 g/1 lb assorted salad leaves
250 g/8 oz yellow teardrop
tomatoes (optional)
250 g/8 oz cherry tomatoes, halved
2 avocados, stoned, peeled and sliced
155 g/5 oz snow peas (mangetout),
trimmed, blanched
250 g/8 oz asparagus spears, cut
into 5 cm/2 in pieces, blanched
3 calamari (squid) tubes
30 g/1 oz butter
250 g/8 oz scallops
16 uncooked medium prawns, shelled
and deveined, tails left intact
200 g/6^1/2 oz thickly sliced smoked
ocean trout or smoked salmon

ORIENTAL DRESSING
1 tablespoon rice vinegar
1 tablespoon fish sauce
2 tablespoons sweet chilli sauce
1 tablespoon shredded fresh basil
1 tablespoon lemon juice
^{1}/4 cup/60 mL/2 fl oz water

This salad is great served warm, but also may be made ahead of time and served chilled. If serving chilled, prepare the salad, seafood and dressing and store separately in the refrigerator. Just prior to serving, assemble the salad as described in the recipe.

1   Arrange salad leaves, teardrop tomatoes (if using) and cherry tomatoes, avocados, snow peas (mangetout) and asparagus on a large serving platter.

2   To make dressing, place vinegar, fish sauce, chilli sauce, basil, lemon juice and water in a small bowl and whisk to combine. Set aside.

3   Cut calamari (squid) tubes, lengthwise, and open out flat. Using a sharp knife, cut parallel lines down the length of the calamari (squid), taking care not to cut right through the flesh. Make more cuts in the opposite direction to form a diamond pattern. Cut each piece into 5 cm/2 in squares.

4   Melt butter in a large frying pan, add scallops and prawns and stir-fry for 3 minutes. Add calamari (squid) pieces and stir-fry for 1 minute longer. Arrange cooked seafood and smoked ocean trout or smoked salmon on salad and drizzle with dressing.

Serves 8

Miniature Passion Fruit Bavarois

This dessert can be made the day before and stored, covered, in the refrigerator.

^{1}/4 cup/60 g/2 oz caster sugar
2 tablespoons Marsala or dry sherry
2 egg yolks
2 teaspoons gelatine
1 tablespoon boiling water
1 egg white
^{1}/4 cup/60 mL/2 fl oz cream
(double), whipped
^{1}/4 cup/60 mL/2 fl oz passion fruit pulp

1   Place sugar, Marsala or sherry and egg yolks in a heatproof bowl set over a saucepan of simmering water. Cook, beating, for 8 minutes or until mixture is thick and leaves a ribbon trail when beaters are lifted from the mixture.

2   Dissolve gelatine in boiling water. Whisk gelatine mixture into custard mixture and set aside to cool. Place egg white in a separate bowl and beat until stiff peaks form. Fold egg white mixture, cream and passion fruit pulp into custard. Spoon mixture into eight oiled small moulds and refrigerate for 3 hours or until set.

Miniature Passion Fruit Bavarois

Serves 8

Plates Limoges Australia

Curry Party

Vegetable Samosa

Spicy Lamb Sticks

Baked Poppadums

Beef Madras

Tandoori Chicken

Vegetable Korma

Spiced Rice

Flatbread

Coriander Chutney

Fruit Pickle

Lemon and Pistachio Pancakes

SERVES 6

Vegetable Samosa

Oven temperature
200°C, 400°F, Gas 6

2 teaspoons vegetable oil
1 tablespoon curry powder
1 onion, finely chopped
1 tablespoon black mustard seeds
2 teaspoons cumin seeds
2 potatoes, finely diced
$^1/_2$ cup/125 mL/4 fl oz vegetable stock
1 carrot, finely diced
125 g/4 oz fresh or frozen peas
500 g/1 lb prepared puff pastry
1 egg, lightly beaten

To cook poppadums, place the required number of poppadums on a baking tray and bake at 180°C/350°F/ Gas 4 for 7-9 minutes or until they are puffed. Some of the poppadums may need to be turned during cooking.

1   Heat oil in a large frying pan over a medium heat. Add curry powder, onion, mustard seeds and cumin seeds and cook, stirring, for 3 minutes.

2   Add potatoes and stock to pan and cook, stirring occasionally, for 5 minutes or until potatoes are tender.

3   Add carrot and peas to pan and cook for 2 minutes longer. Remove pan from heat and set aside to cool completely.

4   Roll out pastry to 5 mm/$^1/_4$ in thick and, using a 10 cm/4 in pastry cutter, cut out twelve rounds. Place spoonfuls of filling on one half of each pastry round, brush edges with egg, fold uncovered half of pastry over filling and press to seal.

5   Place pastries on lightly greased baking trays, brush with remaining egg and bake for 12-15 minutes or until samosa are puffed and golden.

Makes 12

Spicy Lamb Sticks

12 small lamb cutlets, trimmed
of all visible fat

GREEN CURRY MARINADE
2 tablespoons green curry paste
1 clove garlic, crushed
2 tablespoons chopped fresh coriander
2 teaspoons paprika
$^1/_2$ cup/100 g/3$^1/_2$ oz natural yogurt

1   Scrape any meat and fat from exposed bones of cutlets. Place cutlets in a shallow glass or ceramic dish.

2   To make marinade, place curry paste, garlic, coriander, paprika and yogurt in a small bowl and whisk to combine. Spoon marinade over cutlets and turn cutlets to coat with marinade. Cover and stand at room temperature for 1 hour or in the refrigerator overnight.

When removing the cutlets from the marinade do not drain them. They should remain coated with the marinade mixture for cooking.

3   Remove cutlets from dish and cook under a preheated hot grill for 2-4 minutes each side or until cooked to your liking.

Serves 12

Vegetable Samosa,
Spicy Lamb Sticks

SPICED RICE

500 g/1 lb long grain rice
4 coriander seeds
1 cinnamon stick
4 cardamom pods, bruised
90 g/3 oz currants
60 g/2 oz slivered almonds, toasted

1   Bring a large saucepan of water to the boil over a medium heat. Add rice, coriander seeds, cinnamon stick and cardamom pods and boil for 10-12 minutes or until rice is tender.

2   Strain rice and remove spices. Add currants and almonds and mix to combine. Keep warm until ready to serve.

Serves 6

Flatbreads, such as naan, are available from Indian food shops and some supermarkets. All you need to do is heat them before serving.

Beef Madras

1 tablespoon vegetable oil
1.5 kg/3 lb round or topside steak,
trimmed of all visible fat, cut
into 3 cm/1^1/4 in cubes
1^1/4 cups/315 mL/10 fl oz coconut milk
2 cups/500 mL/16 fl oz beef stock

CHILLI PASTE
1 tablespoon coriander seeds
1 tablespoon cumin seeds
2 fresh red chillies, seeded and chopped
12 fresh curry leaves or 6 dried
curry leaves
2 cloves garlic
1 tablespoon lime juice
1 tablespoon brown sugar
3 tablespoons water

1   To make paste, place coriander seeds, cumin seeds, chillies, curry leaves, garlic, lime juice, sugar and water in a food processor or blender and process to make a smooth paste.

2   Heat oil in a large saucepan over a high heat. Add paste and cook, stirring, for 1 minute. Add steak, stir to coat evenly with paste and cook, stirring, for 4 minutes.

3   Add coconut milk and stock to pan and bring to simmering over a medium heat. Simmer, stirring occasionally, for 1 hour or until steak is tender. Add extra stock if curry becomes too dry during cooking.

Serves 6

Fresh curry leaves are available from Indian food shops.

Tandoori Chicken

8 chicken thigh fillets, halved

TANDOORI PASTE
1 cup/200 g/6^1/2 oz natural yogurt
1 tablespoon paprika
3 teaspoons garam masala
1 teaspoon chilli powder
1 tablespoon grated fresh ginger
2 cloves garlic, crushed
2 teaspoons ground cumin

1   To make paste, place yogurt, paprika, garam masala, chilli powder, ginger, garlic and cumin in a bowl and mix to combine.

2   Place chicken in a large shallow glass or ceramic dish. Spoon paste over chicken. Turn to coat with marinade, cover and refrigerate for at least 2 hours.

3   Remove chicken from dish and place on a wire rack set in a baking dish. Pour enough water into baking dish to one-third fill it and bake for 30 minutes or until chicken is cooked and tender.

Serves 6

Oven temperature
200°C, 400°F, Gas 6

As with the Spicy Lamb Sticks, allow the chicken to remain coated with the marinade for cooking.
If chicken thigh fillets are unavailable, chicken breast fillets can be used instead.

Lemon and Pistachio Pancakes
(page 30)

VEGETABLE KORMA

1 tablespoon vegetable oil
2 onions, cut into eighths
1 tablespoon curry paste
2 stalks fresh lemon grass, chopped
or 1 teaspoon dried lemon grass
or 1 teaspoon finely grated lemon rind
1 tablespoon grated fresh ginger
440 g/14 oz canned tomatoes, undrained
and mashed
200 g/6^1/2 oz green beans, trimmed
and halved
250 g/8 oz cauliflower, broken into
small florets
250 g/8 oz broccoli, broken into
small florets
1 red pepper, chopped
1 green pepper, chopped
2 tablespoons chopped fresh mint
200 g/6^1/2 oz unsalted roasted
cashew nuts

1   Heat oil in a large saucepan over a
medium heat. Add onions, curry paste,
lemon grass or lemon rind, and ginger and
cook, stirring, for 3 minutes or until
onions are soft.

2   Add tomatoes, beans, cauliflower,
broccoli, red pepper and green pepper and
cook, stirring occasionally, for 5-6 minutes
or until vegetables are tender. Stir in mint
and cashew nuts. Serve.

Serves 6

This tasty vegetable stew can
be made using whatever
vegetables are available. It
can be made earlier in the
day and reheated over a
medium heat or in the
microwave just prior to
serving.

CORIANDER CHUTNEY

1 large bunch fresh coriander,
roots removed
4 tablespoons desiccated coconut
2 tablespoons lemon juice
2 tablespoons water
2 fresh red chillies, seeded and chopped
$^1/_2$ teaspoon ground cardamom

Place coriander leaves and stems, coconut, lemon juice, water, chillies and cardamom in a food processor or blender and process until finely chopped. Store in an airtight container in the refrigerator.

Makes $^3/_4$ cup/185 g/6 oz

FRUIT PICKLE

90 g/3 oz sultanas
60 g/2 oz chopped dried apricots
60 g/2 oz chopped dried dates
1 cup/250 mL/8 fl oz water
2 cinnamon sticks
3 cloves
$^1/_2$ cup/125 mL/4 fl oz vinegar
$^1/_2$ cup/90 g/3 oz brown sugar
1 tablespoon sliced fresh ginger

Rather than make your own chutney and pickle, you could serve purchased ones. There are many good chutneys and relishes available from supermarkets and Indian food shops.

Place sultanas, apricots, dates, water, cinnamon sticks, cloves, vinegar, sugar and ginger in a saucepan and cook over a low heat, stirring frequently, for 30 minutes or until mixture reduces and thickens. Remove cinnamon sticks. Store pickle in an airtight container in the refrigerator.

Makes 1 cup/250 g/8 oz

LEMON AND PISTACHIO PANCAKES

1 cup/125 g/4 oz self-raising flour
$^1/_4$ cup/60 g/2 oz sugar
250 g/8 oz natural yogurt
1 egg, lightly beaten
$^1/_3$ cup/90 mL/3 fl oz milk
1 tablespoon finely grated lemon rind
60 g/2 oz chopped pistachio nuts

1   Place flour and sugar in a bowl and mix to combine. Whisk in yogurt, egg, milk, lemon rind and pistachio nuts and continue whisking until batter is smooth.

2   Cook dessertspoonfuls of mixture in a heated, greased, heavy-based frying pan for 1-2 minutes or until bubbles form on the surface, then turn and cook for 1-2 minutes longer or until golden. Serve immediately.

Serve pancakes stacked, with whipped cream and extra pistachios.

Serves 6

Candlelight Dinner

Avocado Tahini Toasts
Smoked Salmon Soufflés

Fillet of Beef with Salsa Verde
Potato Tarts
Asparagus with Browned Butter

Berry Mousses

SERVES 2

AVOCADO TAHINI TOASTS

6 slices white bread, crusts removed
1 avocado, stoned, peeled and sliced

TAHINI SAUCE
3 tablespoons natural yogurt
1 tablespoon tahini paste
1/4 teaspoon ground cumin
1/4 teaspoon ground coriander
1 teaspoon lemon juice

1   Using a round or star-shaped biscuit cutter, cut bread into six shapes. Cook bread under a preheated medium grill for 1-2 minutes each side or until golden.

2   To make sauce, place yogurt, tahini paste, cumin, coriander and lemon juice in a small bowl and mix until smooth.

3   Top toasts with avocado slices and sauce. Serve immediately.

Serves 2

The Tahini Sauce can be made in advance and stored, covered, in the refrigerator. But leave toasting the bread, cutting the avocado and assembling to just prior to serving.

SMOKED SALMON SOUFFLES

45 g/1 1/2 oz grated Parmesan cheese
15 g/1/2 oz butter
2 tablespoons flour
1/2 cup/125 mL/4 fl oz milk
1/4 cup/60 mL/2 fl oz cream (double)
3 eggs, separated
60 g/2 oz grated Gruyère cheese
60 g/2 oz smoked salmon, shredded
1 tablespoon chopped fresh dill

1   Grease two 1 cup/250 mL/8 fl oz capacity ramekins and sprinkle base and sides with 30 g/1 oz Parmesan cheese.

2   Melt butter in a small saucepan over a medium heat. Stir in flour and cook for 2 minutes. Remove pan from heat and gradually whisk in milk and cream.

3   Return pan to heat and cook, stirring constantly, for 4 minutes or until sauce boils and thickens. Remove pan from heat and set aside to cool slightly.

4   Add egg yolks, Gruyère cheese, remaining Parmesan cheese, salmon and dill to sauce and mix to combine.

5   Place egg whites in a bowl and beat until stiff peaks form. Fold egg white mixture into salmon mixture. Pour soufflé mixture into ramekins and bake for 20-25 minutes or until soufflés are puffed and golden. Serve immediately.

Serves 2

Oven temperature
180°C, 350°F, Gas 4

This recipe can be completed to the end of step 4, several hours in advance. If making in advance, allow the sauce mixture to cool slightly, then place plastic food wrap directly on top of the mixture – this will prevent a skin forming.

Avocado Tahini Toasts,
Smoked Salmon Soufflés

FILLET OF BEEF WITH SALSA VERDE

Oven temperature
190°C, 375°F, Gas 5

500 g/1 lb beef fillet, trimmed of all
visible fat and sinew
3 tablespoons wholegrain mustard
1 tablespoon crushed black peppercorns
1 tablespoon black mustard seeds,
crushed
1 tablespoon vegetable oil

SALSA VERDE
1 bunch flat-leaved parsley
2 teaspoons capers, drained
1 clove garlic, crushed
2 canned anchovies, drained
1 tablespoon lemon juice
2 slices bread, crusts trimmed
$^1/_4$ cup/60 mL/2 fl oz olive oil

1   Spread beef with mustard, then roll in
black pepper and mustard seeds.

2   Heat oil in a large frying pan, add beef
and cook, turning, until browned on all
sides. Place beef in a baking dish and
bake for 35-40 minutes or until cooked to
your liking.

3   To make Salsa Verde, place parsley,
capers, garlic, anchovies, lemon juice
and bread in a food processor or blender
and process until finely chopped. With
machine running, slowly add oil and
continue processing to make a thick
paste.

4   To serve, slice beef and accompany
with Salsa Verde.

Serves 2

The salsa can be made 2-3
days in advance and stored
in an airtight container in the
refrigerator. Bring to room
temperature and mix to
combine before serving.

POTATO TARTS

Oven temperature
180°C, 350°F, Gas 4

2 large potatoes, thinly sliced
1 onion, thinly sliced
$^1/_4$ cup/60 g/2 oz sour cream
$^1/_4$ cup/60 mL/2 fl oz milk
1 teaspoon crushed black peppercorns

1   Arrange potatoes and onions in layers
in two greased 1 cup/250 mL/8 fl oz
capacity ramekins.

2   Place sour cream, milk and black
pepper in a bowl and mix to combine.
Pour sour cream mixture over potatoes
and bake for 30 minutes or until potatoes
are tender and top is golden.

Serves 2

*Potato Tarts, Asparagus with Browned
Butter, Fillet of Beef with Salsa Verde*

ASPARAGUS WITH BROWNED BUTTER

8 asparagus spears, trimmed
45 g/1¹/₂ oz butter

1 Boil, steam or microwave asparagus until tender.

2 Place butter in a small saucepan and cook over a low heat until browned. Pour butter over asparagus and serve immediately.

Serves 2

If fresh asparagus is unavailable, this is also a delicious way to serve green beans.

BERRY MOUSSES

100 g/3^1/$_2$ oz blueberries
100 g/3^1/$_2$ oz raspberries
100 g/3^1/$_2$ oz mulberries
2 tablespoons maple or golden syrup
1 cup/250 mL/8 fl oz cream
(double), whipped
2 egg whites
3 teaspoons gelatine dissolved in
1 tablespoon boiling water, cooled

CHOCOLATE CREAM
90 g/3 oz chocolate, melted and cooled
^{1}/$_4$ cup/60 mL/2 fl oz cream (double)

The mousses and Chocolate Cream can be made the day before. Remove the Chocolate Cream from the refrigerator 1 hour prior to serving to allow it to soften. Any combination of fresh, canned or frozen berries can be used for this dessert. If using canned berries, drain them well first. If using frozen berries allow them to thaw before using.

1   Place blueberries, raspberries, mulberries and maple or golden syrup in a food processor or blender and process until smooth. Push purée through a fine sieve to remove seeds. Place egg whites in a bowl and beat until stiff peaks form.

2   Fold berry mixture into whipped cream, then fold in egg whites and gelatine mixture. Carefully pour mixture into two oiled ^{3}/4 cup/185 mL/6 fl oz capacity moulds or ramekins. Cover and refrigerate for 2 hours or until set.

3   To make Chocolate Cream, fold chocolate into cream. To serve, unmould mousses, place on serving plates and accompany with Chocolate Cream.

Berry Mousses

Serves 2

Healthy Celebration

Asparagus and Salmon Salad

Char-grilled Tarragon Chicken

Warm Potato Salad

Mixed Tomato Salad

Angels' Brownies with Fruit

SERVES 6

ASPARAGUS AND SALMON SALAD

750 g/1 1/2 lb asparagus spears, trimmed
lettuce leaves of your choice
500 g/1 1b smoked salmon slices
freshly ground black pepper

LEMON YOGURT SAUCE
1 cup/200 g/6 1/2 oz natural
low-fat yogurt
1 tablespoon finely grated lemon rind
1 tablespoon lemon juice
1 tablespoon chopped fresh dill
1 teaspoon ground cumin

Serves 6

1   Boil, steam or microwave asparagus until tender. Drain, refresh under cold running water, drain again and chill. Arrange lettuce leaves, asparagus and salmon on serving plates.

2   To make sauce, place yogurt, lemon rind, lemon juice, dill and cumin in a small bowl and mix to combine.

3   Spoon sauce over salad. Sprinkle with black pepper, cover and chill until required.

If fresh asparagus is unavailable, green beans or snow peas (mangetout) are good alternatives for this recipe.

Plates Limoges Australia Napkin and cloth In Residence

38

Char-grilled Tarragon Chicken

Left: Asparagus and Salmon Salad
Above: Char-grilled Tarragon
Chicken, Warm Potato Salad
(page 40), Mixed Tomato Salad
(page 40)

6 boneless chicken breast fillets,
skin removed
3 tablespoons chopped fresh tarragon or
2 teaspoons dried tarragon
1 cup/250 mL/8 fl oz dry white wine
2 tablespoons lemon rind strips
1 tablespoon green peppercorns in brine,
drained and crushed

1   Place chicken in a single layer in a shallow glass or ceramic dish. Combine tarragon, wine, lemon rind and green peppercorns. Pour marinade over chicken. Turn to coat chicken with marinade and marinate at room temperature, turning once, for 20 minutes.

2   Remove chicken from marinade and cook on a preheated hot char grill or in a preheated grill pan for 5 minutes or until tender.

Serves 6

Do not marinate chicken any longer than 20 minutes as the marinade will cause the chicken to break down.
As an alternative to cooking the chicken on a char grill you can cook it under a preheated hot grill.

Warm Potato Salad

1 kg/2 lb baby new potatoes, quartered
freshly ground black pepper

HERB DRESSING
1 tablespoon capers, drained
and chopped
1 tablespoon chopped fresh parsley
1 tablespoon chopped fresh basil
2 tablespoons white wine vinegar
2 tablespoons vegetable oil

1   Cook potatoes in a saucepan of boiling water for 6 minutes or until just tender, then drain and place in a heatproof serving bowl.

2   To make dressing, place capers, parsley, basil, vinegar and oil in a small bowl and whisk to combine.

3   Pour dressing over warm potatoes, toss to coat and sprinkle generously with black pepper. Serve warm.

Serves 6

Mixed Tomato Salad

250 g/8 oz cherry tomatoes, halved
2 ox heart (beefsteak) tomatoes,
cut into wedges
4 plum (egg or Italian)
tomatoes, quartered
1 red onion, chopped
2 tablespoons balsamic or
red wine vinegar
1 tablespoon chopped fresh thyme
freshly ground black pepper

1   Place cherry, ox heart (beefsteak) and plum (egg or Italian) tomatoes in a serving dish. Add onion, vinegar, thyme and black pepper to taste. Toss to combine.

2   Cover and chill for at least 1 hour before serving.

Serves 6

If plum (egg or Italian) tomatoes are not available, use ordinary tomatoes cut into wedges or increase the quantity of cherry tomatoes.

Angels' Brownies with Fruit

ANGELS' BROWNIES WITH FRUIT

sliced fresh fruit
low-fat vanilla yogurt

ANGELS' BROWNIES
³/4 cup/90 g/3 oz flour
¹/2 teaspoon baking powder
¹/2 cup/45 g/1¹/2 oz cocoa powder
1 cup/220 g/7 oz caster sugar
¹/2 cup/100 g/3¹/2 oz low-fat
vanilla yogurt
2 eggs
1 teaspoon vanilla essence
1¹/2 tablespoons vegetable oil

1   To make brownies, sift flour, baking powder and cocoa powder together into a bowl. Add sugar, yogurt, eggs, vanilla essence and oil and mix to combine.

2   Pour batter into a 20 cm/8 in square cake tin lined with nonstick baking paper and bake for 25-30 minutes or until brownies are firm.

3   Allow brownies to cool in tin. Cut into squares and serve with fresh fruit and vanilla yogurt.

Makes 16 brownies

Oven temperature
180°C, 350°F, Gas 4

Leftover brownies will keep in an airtight container in the refrigerator for several days and are delicious for afternoon tea or in a packed lunch.

41

Family Dinner

Spicy Pumpkin Soup

Herb Damper

Apple and Sage Pork Roast

Apple Sauce

Honeyed Roast Vegetables

Steamed Green Vegetables
of Your Choice

Sticky Banana Pudding

SERVES 10

SPICY PUMPKIN SOUP

1.5 kg/3 lb pumpkin flesh, chopped
6 cups/1.5 litres/2^1/$_2$ pt chicken stock
1 teaspoon ground cumin
1 teaspoon chilli powder
1^1/$_2$ cups/375 mL/12 fl oz
cream (double)
4 tablespoons snipped fresh chives
^{1}/$_4$ cup/60 mL/2 fl oz brandy
1 teaspoon grated nutmeg
freshly ground black pepper

1   Place pumpkin and stock in a large saucepan, bring to simmering over a medium heat and cook for 20 minutes or until pumpkin is tender. Remove pan from heat and set aside to cool slightly.

2   Place pumpkin and stock in batches in a food processor or blender and process until smooth.

3   Return mixture to a clean pan. Stir in cumin, chilli powder and cream and bring to simmering over a medium heat, stirring occasionally. Simmer for 3-5 minutes or until heated through. Stir in chives, brandy and nutmeg and season to taste with black pepper. Serve with warm Herb Damper.

Serves 10

This soup can be made the day before and reheated when required.
You may prefer to make this recipe using carrots instead of pumpkin. Simply replace the pumpkin with the same quantity of prepared carrots.

HERB DAMPER

3 cups/375 g/12 oz self-raising flour
45 g/1^1/$_2$ oz butter
1 tablespoon chopped fresh basil
1 tablespoon snipped fresh chives
1 tablespoon chopped fresh parsley
^{1}/$_2$ cup/125 mL/4 fl oz milk
^{3}/$_4$ cup/185 mL/6 fl oz water

1   Place flour in a bowl and rub in butter using fingertips until mixture resembles coarse breadcrumbs.

2   Stir in basil, chives, parsley, milk and enough water to form a soft dough. Turn dough onto a lightly floured surface and knead until smooth.

3   Shape dough into a large round, place on a greased baking tray and bake for 40 minutes or until cooked. Serve warm.

Serves 10

Oven temperature
180°C, 350°F, Gas 4

To test if the damper is cooked, tap the base with your fingers. If it sounds hollow it is cooked.

Herb Damper, Spicy Pumpkin Soup

APPLE SAUCE

1 cup/250 mL/8 fl oz apple juice
¹/₂ cup/125 mL/4 fl oz dry white wine
¹/₂ cup/125 mL/4 fl oz beef stock
6 fresh sage leaves or ¹/₂ teaspoon
dried sage
¹/₂ cup/125 g/4 oz sour cream
freshly ground black pepper

1   Place apple juice, wine, stock and sage in a saucepan, bring to simmering over a low heat and simmer, stirring, for 5 minutes or until mixture reduces by half.

2   Remove pan from heat and remove sage leaves (if using fresh sage). Gradually whisk in sour cream and season to taste with black pepper.

Serves 10

This sauce can be made in advance and reheated. It can be reheated in the microwave or in a saucepan over a low heat. Take care not to heat it for too long or it may curdle.

APPLE AND SAGE PORK ROAST

Oven temperature
180°C, 350°F, Gas 4

2 x 1-1.5 kg/2-3 lb pork loins

APPLE AND SAGE STUFFING
15 g/^{1}/$_2$ oz butter
^{1}/$_4$ cup/45 g/1^1/$_2$ oz brown sugar
1 teaspoon ground cinnamon
2 apples, cored, peeled and sliced
3 cups/185 g/6 oz breadcrumbs,
made from stale bread
4 tablespoons chopped fresh sage
or 2 teaspoons dried sage
1 egg, lightly beaten
1 teaspoon crushed black peppercorns

When scoring pork rind take care not to cut too deeply. The cuts should only be about 5 mm/^{1}/$_4$ in deep. Scoring makes the rind easier to cut when cooked.

1   Unroll pork loins, make a cut in the middle of the fleshy part of the meat and lay out. Using a sharp knife, score rind at 2 cm/^{3}/$_4$ in intervals. Set aside.

2   To make stuffing, place butter, sugar and cinnamon in a frying pan and cook over a medium heat, stirring constantly, for 2 minutes or until mixture is syrupy.

3   Add apple slices to pan and cook for 1 minute each side or until golden.

4   Place breadcrumbs, sage, egg and black pepper in a bowl and mix to combine.

5   Place pork rind side down and place a layer of apples over flesh, leaving a 2 cm/^{3}/$_4$ in border. Top with a layer of breadcrumb mixture. Roll pork loins and tie with string.

6   Place rolled loins on a wire rack set in a baking dish and bake for 1 hour or until tender. To serve, slice pork and accompany with Apple Sauce.

Serves 10

HONEYED ROAST VEGETABLES

Oven temperature
200°C, 400°F, Gas 6

20 pieces pumpkin or 10 carrots,
halved lengthwise
10 pieces sweet potato
5 onions, halved
5 small parsnips, halved
4 tablespoons honey, warmed

1   Place pumpkin or carrots, sweet potato, onions and parsnips in a well-greased baking dish and bake for 40-50 minutes or until vegetables are almost cooked.

2   Brush vegetables with honey and bake for 10 minutes longer or until golden.

Serves 10

Sticky Banana Pudding

STICKY BANANA PUDDING

375 g/12 oz butter, softened
1^1/2 cups/330 g/10^1/2 oz caster sugar
6 eggs
3 cups/375 g/12 oz self-raising flour
1^1/2 teaspoons baking powder
1 teaspoon cinnamon
1 teaspoon vanilla essence
3 large bananas, mashed

TOFFEE SAUCE
220 g/7 oz butter
1^1/4 cups/220 g/7 oz brown sugar
1^3/4 cups/440 mL/14 fl oz
cream (double)

Oven temperature
180°C, 350°F, Gas 4

1   Place butter and caster sugar in a bowl and beat until light and creamy. Add eggs one at a time, beating well after each addition.

2   Sift together flour, baking powder and cinnamon. Fold flour mixture and vanilla essence into butter mixture. Stir in bananas. Pour batter into a greased and lined 25 cm/10 in square cake tin and bake for 1 hour or until cooked when tested with a skewer.

3   To make sauce, place butter and brown sugar in a saucepan and cook over a low heat, stirring, for 10 minutes or until sugar dissolves. Remove pan from heat and gradually stir in cream. Return pan to heat, bring to simmering and simmer, stirring, for 4 minutes until sauce is smooth.

4   Serve pudding hot or warm, cut into squares and accompanied by sauce.

Serves 10

Thai Influence

Sweet Chilli Parcels
Curry Puffs with Minted Yogurt
Thai Fish Cakes

Prawn Satays
Chicken with Lemon Grass
Thai Beef Salad
Red Curry Vegetables
Jasmine or Basmati Rice

Ice Cream of Your Choice
or
Selection of Fresh Fruit

SERVES 8

SWEET CHILLI PARCELS

200 g/6¹/₂ oz pork mince
4 spring onions, chopped
1 carrot, grated
2 tablespoons soy sauce
3 tablespoons crunchy peanut butter
24 spring roll or wonton wrappers, each
12.5 cm/5 in square
vegetable oil for deep-frying
sweet chilli sauce

The uncooked parcels can be prepared the day before and stored, covered, in the refrigerator until required. Spring roll or wonton wrappers are available frozen from Asian food shops and some supermarkets.

1 Heat a nonstick frying pan over a high heat, add pork and cook, stirring, for 5 minutes or until browned.

2 Add spring onions, carrot, soy sauce and peanut butter to pan and cook, stirring, for 2 minutes longer. Remove pan from heat and set aside to cool completely.

3 Place spoonfuls of mixture in the centre of each spring roll or wonton wrapper, then draw the corners together and twist to form small bundles.

4 Heat oil in a large saucepan until a cube of bread dropped in browns in 50 seconds. Cook bundles a few at a time for 3-4 minutes or until golden. Drain and serve with sweet chilli sauce.

Makes 16

THAI FISH CAKES

500 g/1 lb boneless firm white fish
fillets, skinned
3 spring onions, chopped
1 egg, lightly beaten
2 tablespoons flour
2 fresh red chillies, seeded and chopped
¹/₂ teaspoon cumin seeds
2 teaspoons grated fresh ginger
vegetable oil for shallow-frying

CORIANDER CHUTNEY
1 bunch fresh coriander
4 spring onions, chopped
1 tablespoon grated fresh ginger
1 clove garlic, crushed
2 tablespoons lime or lemon juice
1 tablespoon vegetable oil

The fish cakes can be prepared the day before and stored, covered, in the refrigerator. Cook just prior to serving. The chutney can also be made the day before and stored in an airtight container in the refrigerator.

1 Place fish in a food processor and process to finely chopped. Add spring onions, egg, flour, chillies, cumin seeds and ginger and process to make a stiff paste.

2 Take 2 tablespoons of fish mixture and shape into a small flat cake. Place on a plate lined with plastic food wrap. Repeat with remaining mixture.

3 Heat oil in a frying pan over a medium heat and cook fish cakes a few at a time for 3-4 minutes each side or until cooked.

4 To make chutney, place coriander leaves and stems, spring onions, ginger, garlic, lime or lemon juice and oil in a food processor or blender and process until smooth. Serve chutney with fish cakes.

Makes 16

Thai Fish Cakes, Curry Puffs with Minted Yogurt, Sweet Chilli Parcels

CURRY PUFFS WITH MINTED YOGURT

1 teaspoon ground cumin
1 teaspoon ground coriander
2 teaspoons mild curry paste
2 onions, chopped
250 g/8 oz lamb or beef mince
500 g/1 lb prepared puff pastry

MINTED YOGURT
1 cup/200 g/6^1/$_2$ oz natural yogurt
4 tablespoons chopped fresh mint
1 teaspoon ground cumin

1   Place cumin and coriander in a nonstick frying pan and cook over a high heat, stirring, for 1 minute. Add curry paste and onions and cook, stirring for 2 minutes longer.

2   Add lamb or beef and cook, stirring, for 4 minutes or until browned. Remove pan from heat and set aside to cool.

3   Roll out pastry to 3 mm/^{1}/$_8$ in thick and, using a 5 cm/2 in round pastry cutter, cut out sixteen circles. Place a spoonful of meat mixture on one half of each pastry circle. Fold pastry over to encase meat mixture, then press edges together with a fork to seal.

4   Place pastries on a lightly greased baking tray and bake for 10-12 minutes or until golden brown.

5   To make Minted Yogurt, place yogurt, mint and cumin in a small bowl and mix to combine. Serve with warm Curry Puffs.

Makes 16

Oven temperature
180°C, 350°F, Gas 4

The filling for the Curry Puffs can be made the day before it is required and stored, covered, in the refrigerator.

PRAWN SATAYS

1 kg/2 lb uncooked large prawns, shelled
and deveined, tails left intact

SATAY SAUCE
2 teaspoons vegetable oil
1 onion, chopped
3 teaspoons ground cumin
1 cup/265 g/8$^{1}/_{2}$ oz crunchy
peanut butter
1 cup/250 mL/8 fl oz chicken stock
3 tablespoons soy sauce

1   Thread prawns onto eight skewers.

2   To make sauce, heat oil in a saucepan,
add onion and cumin and cook, stirring,
for 3 minutes or until onion is soft.

3   Add peanut butter, stock and soy
sauce and cook over a medium heat,
stirring, for 5 minutes or until sauce boils
and thickens.

4   Brush prawns with sauce and cook
under a preheated hot grill for 2 minutes
each side or until prawns change colour
and are cooked. To serve, drizzle with any
remaining sauce.

Makes 8

The sauce can be prepared
the day before and stored in
an airtight container in the
refrigerator. Before using,
heat over a low heat, stirring,
or in a microwave.

CHICKEN WITH LEMON GRASS

2 teaspoons vegetable oil
4 boneless chicken breast fillets,
cut into strips
2 stalks fresh lemon grass, chopped
or 1 teaspoon dried lemon grass
$^{1}/_{2}$ cup/125 mL/4 fl oz coconut milk
2 teaspoons finely grated lime rind
2 tablespoons lime juice
3 tablespoons shredded fresh basil
3 tablespoons sweet chilli sauce
6 spring onions, sliced diagonally
2 tablespoons chopped fresh coriander

1   Heat a wok or large frying pan over a
high heat. Add oil and chicken and stir-
fry for 3-5 minutes or until chicken
changes colour.

2   Add lemon grass, coconut milk, lime
rind, lime juice, basil, chilli sauce, spring
onions and coriander and stir-fry for 2
minutes longer or until chicken is
cooked. Serve immediately.

Serves 8

If lemon grass is unavailable
you can use 1 teaspoon
finely grated lemon rind in
its place.

THAI BEEF SALAD

1 kg/2 lb rump steak, trimmed
of all visible fat
375 g/12 oz assorted salad greens
1 cucumber, peeled and sliced
1 red pepper, thinly sliced

CHILLI MARINADE
$^1/_3$ cup/90 mL/3 fl oz soy sauce
2 tablespoons sweet chilli sauce
2 tablespoons chopped fresh coriander
1 teaspoon crushed black peppercorns

1   Cut steak into long thin strips.

2   To make marinade, place soy sauce, chilli sauce, coriander and black pepper in a bowl and mix to combine. Add steak, toss to coat with marinade, cover and refrigerate for 2 hours.

3   Arrange salad greens, cucumber and red pepper on a serving platter. Set aside.

4   Drain meat and reserve marinade. Heat a nonstick frying pan over a high heat, add steak and stir-fry for 1 minute. Arrange meat on salad.

5   Add marinade to pan and cook, stirring, for 2 minutes or until marinade reduces slightly. Spoon over salad and serve immediately.

Serves 8

This salad makes a delicious main course for a special summer lunch party. If serving as the main dish, this recipe would serve 4.

RED CURRY VEGETABLES

2-3 tablespoons red curry paste,
or according to taste
4 potatoes, chopped
300 g/9$^1/_2$ oz pumpkin or
carrots, chopped
400 g/12$^1/_2$ oz sweet potatoes, chopped
2 cups/500 mL/16 fl oz vegetable stock
300 g/9$^1/_2$ oz cauliflower, broken
into small florets
250 g/8 oz green beans, trimmed

1   Place curry paste in a large saucepan and cook over a medium heat, stirring, for 2 minutes.

2   Add potatoes, pumpkin or carrrots, sweet potatoes and vegetable stock and bring to simmering. Simmer, stirring occasionally, for 20 minutes or until vegetables are almost cooked.

3   Add cauliflower and beans and cook for 3-5 minutes longer or until vegetables are tender. Serve immediately.

Serves 8

Use whatever vegetables are available for this curry. Broccoli, zucchini (courgettes) and eggplant (aubergines) are other vegetables you might like to include.

Stylish Vegetarian

Roasted Eggplant Soup
Brie and Sage Toasts

Wild Mushroom Pizza
Watercress and Avocado Pizza
Mixed Greens

Coconut and Raspberry Cake

SERVES 6

ROASTED EGGPLANT SOUP

1 kg/2 lb eggplant (aubergines), halved
4 red peppers, halved
1 teaspoon olive oil
2 cloves garlic, crushed
4 tomatoes, peeled and chopped
3 cups/750 mL/1 1/4 pt vegetable stock
2 teaspoons crushed black peppercorns

This soup can be made the day before and reheated when required.

1   Place eggplant (aubergines) and red peppers, skin side up under a preheated hot grill and cook for 10 minutes or until flesh is soft and skins are blackened. Peel away blackened skin and roughly chop flesh.

2   Heat oil in a large saucepan over a medium heat. Add garlic and tomatoes and cook, stirring, for 2 minutes. Add eggplant (aubergines), red peppers, stock and black pepper, bring to simmering and simmer for 4 minutes. Remove pan from heat and set aside to cool slightly.

3   Place vegetables and stock in batches in food processor or blender and process until smooth. Return mixture to a clean pan, bring to simmering over a medium heat and simmer for 3-5 minutes or until heated through.

Serves 6

MIXED GREENS

375 g/12 oz mixed lettuce leaves, torn into large pieces
8 English spinach leaves, shredded
90 g/3 oz rocket or watercress leaves

BASIL DRESSING
1/4 cup/60 mL/2 fl oz red wine vinegar
1/4 cup/60 mL/2 fl oz olive oil
2 teaspoons finely grated lime or lemon rind
1 tablespoon chopped fresh basil
1 teaspoon crushed black peppercorns

1   Arrange lettuce leaves, spinach and rocket or watercress in a serving bowl. Cover and chill.

2   To make dressing, place vinegar, oil, lime or lemon rind, basil and black pepper in a screwtop jar and shake to combine. Just prior to serving, pour dressing over salad and toss.

Serves 6

BRIE AND SAGE TOASTS

Roasted Eggplant Soup,
Brie and Sage Toasts

**12 small bread rounds, toasted
200 g/6¹/₂ oz Brie, sliced
fresh sage leaves**

Top toasts with Brie and sage leaves.
Place under a preheated hot grill and
cook for 1-2 minutes or until cheese just
melts. Serve hot with soup.

Makes 12

You can either purchase the
bread rounds or make them
yourself. To make, cut rounds
from thin slices of bread,
using a 2.5 cm/1 in biscuit
cutter.

WATERCRESS AND AVOCADO PIZZA

^{1}/$_2$ cup/125 g/4 oz crème fraiche or
sour cream
100 g/3^1/$_2$ oz watercress leaves
1 fresh red chilli, chopped
1 large pizza base, purchased or
homemade (see recipe)
2 avocados, stoned, peeled and sliced
8 sun-dried tomatoes, chopped
125 g/4 oz creamy blue cheese,
crumbled
100 g/3^1/$_2$ oz grated tasty cheese
(mature Cheddar)

1   Place crème fraiche or sour cream,
watercress and chilli in a small bowl and
mix to combine. Spread over pizza base
and bake for 15 minutes.

2   Remove pizza from oven and top with
avocado slices and sun-dried tomatoes.
Combine blue cheese and tasty cheese
(mature Cheddar) and sprinkle over pizza.

3   Reduce oven temperature to 190°C/
375°F/Gas 5, return pizza to oven and
bake for 10 minutes longer or until cheese
melts and is golden.

Serves 6

WILD MUSHROOM PIZZA

45 g/1^1/$_2$ oz butter
2 onions, sliced
2 tablespoons brown sugar
1 tablespoon fresh thyme leaves
or 1 teaspoon dried thyme
1 large pizza base, purchased or
homemade (see recipe)
125 g/4 oz button mushrooms
125 g/4 oz oyster mushrooms
125 g/4 oz shiitake mushrooms
200 g/6^1/$_2$ oz wild mushrooms
of your choice
4 tablespoons grated Parmesan cheese
2 teaspoons crushed black peppercorns

1   Heat 15 g/^{1}/$_2$ oz butter in a frying pan
over a medium heat until foaming. Add
onions and cook over a low heat, stirring,
for 10-15 minutes or until golden. Add
sugar and thyme and cook, stirring, for 2
minutes longer. Spread onion mixture
over pizza base.

2   Heat remaining butter in frying pan,
add button, oyster, shiitake and wild
mushrooms and cook, stirring, for 2
minutes.

3   Spread mushroom mixture over
onions, sprinkle with Parmesan cheese
and black pepper and bake for 15
minutes. Reduce oven temperature to
190°C/375°F/Gas 5 and cook for 10
minutes longer.

Serves 6

Coconut and Raspberry Cake

COCONUT AND RASPBERRY CAKE

200 g/6¹/₂ oz fresh or frozen raspberries
1¹/₂ cups/375 mL/12 fl oz cream
(double), whipped
90 g/3 oz shredded coconut, toasted

COCONUT CAKE
185 g/6 oz butter, softened
1 cup/220 g/7 oz caster sugar
4 eggs, separated
90 g/3 oz desiccated coconut
3 cups/375 g/12 oz self-raising flour
1 teaspoon baking powder
1 teaspoon vanilla essence
³/₄ cup/185 mL/6 fl oz coconut milk

RASPBERRY COULIS
500 g/1 lb fresh or frozen raspberries
2 tablespoons icing sugar

1   To make cake, place butter and sugar in a bowl and beat until light and creamy. Add egg yolks one at a time, beating well after each addition. Fold in coconut.

2   Sift flour and baking powder together. Combine vanilla essence and coconut milk. Fold flour mixture and coconut milk mixture, alternately, into butter mixture. Place egg whites in a bowl and beat until stiff peaks form. Fold egg white mixture into batter.

3   Pour batter into two greased and floured 20 cm/8 in square cake tins and bake for 35-40 minutes or until cake comes away from sides of tin. Stand cakes in tins for 5 minutes before turning onto wire racks to cool.

4   To assemble, top one cake with raspberries, then with remaining cake. Spread top and sides of cake with cream and sprinkle with coconut. Refrigerate until ready to serve.

5   To make coulis, place raspberries and icing sugar in a food processor or blender and process to purée. Press purée through a sieve to remove seeds. Serve with cake.

Makes a 20 cm/8 in square cake

Oven temperature
180°C, 350°F, Gas 4

The cake can be made the day before and stored in an airtight container. Assemble the cake up to 4 hours before serving. Make the coulis the day before and store, covered, in the refrigerator.

Summer Affair

Prawns with Creamy Pesto Dip

Drunken Sirloin Steaks

Glazed Onions

Rosemary Baked Potatoes

BLT Salad

Peach Cheesecake

SERVES 8

PRAWNS WITH CREAMY PESTO DIP

1 kg/2 lb cooked medium prawns,
shelled and deveined, tails left intact
2 carrots, cut into thick strips
200 g/6$^{1}/_{2}$ oz snow peas (mangetout),
blanched
1 red pepper, cut into thick strips

CREAMY PESTO DIP
$^{1}/_{2}$ cup/125 g/4 oz ready-made pesto
$^{1}/_{2}$ cup/125 mL/4 fl oz whole
egg mayonnaise

1   To make dip, place pesto and
mayonnaise in a bowl and mix to
combine.

2   To serve, place dip in a small bowl on
a large serving platter and surround with
prawns, carrots, snow peas (mangetout)
and red pepper.

Serves 8

This dish can be prepared
several hours in advance
and stored, covered, in the
refrigerator until required.
Ready-made pesto is
available from Italian
delicatessens and some
supermarkets.

DRUNKEN SIRLOIN STEAKS

8 sirloin steaks, trimmed of all visible fat

DRUNKEN MARINADE
$^{3}/_{4}$ cup/185 mL/6 fl oz beer
2 cloves garlic, crushed
$^{1}/_{4}$ cup/60 mL/2 fl oz Worcestershire
sauce
$^{1}/_{4}$ cup/60 mL/2 fl oz tomato sauce

1   To make marinade, place beer, garlic,
Worcestershire sauce and tomato sauce in
a large shallow glass or ceramic dish and
mix to combine.

2   Add steaks to marinade, turn to coat,
cover and set aside to marinate at room
temperature for at least 3 hours or in the
refrigerator overnight. Turn occasionally
during marinating.

3   Preheat barbecue to hot. Drain steaks
and reserve marinade. Cook steaks on
lightly oiled barbecue, brushing with
reserved marinade, for 3-5 minutes each
side or until cooked to your liking. Serve
immediately.

Serves 8

When testing to see if a steak
is cooked to your liking, press
it with a pair of blunt tongs.
Do not cut the meat, as this
causes the juices to escape.
Rare steaks will feel springy,
medium slightly springy and
well-done will feel firm.

Prawns with Creamy Pesto Dip

BLT Salad

5 rashers bacon, chopped
1 cos lettuce, torn into large pieces
1 mignonette (lollo rosso) lettuce, torn into large pieces
3 tomatoes, cut into wedges
fresh Parmesan cheese

YOGURT DRESSING
$^1/_2$ cup/100 g/$3^1/_2$ oz natural yogurt
2 tablespoons lemon juice
1 tablespoon wholegrain mustard
1 teaspoon crushed black peppercorns
1 tablespoon vegetable oil

1 Cook bacon in a frying pan over medium heat for 4 minutes or until crisp. Remove bacon from pan and drain on absorbent kitchen paper.

2 Place cos and mignonette (lollo rosso) lettuce, tomatoes and bacon in a large salad bowl.

3 To make dressing, place yogurt, lemon juice, mustard, black pepper and oil in a bowl and whisk to combine. Pour dressing over salad, cover and chill. Just prior to serving, top with shavings of Parmesan cheese.

Serves 8

To make shavings of Parmesan cheese you will need a piece of fresh Parmesan cheese. Use a vegetable peeler or a coarse grater to remove shavings from the cheese.

Glazed Onions

3 onions, sliced
1 tablespoon vegetable oil
2 tablespoons honey
1 tablespoon vinegar

1   Preheat barbecue to hot. Place onions and oil in a bowl and mix to combine. Place onion mixture on lightly oiled barbecue plate (griddle) or in a lightly oiled frying pan on barbecue and cook, stirring, for 2-5 minutes or until onions are tender.

2   Add honey and vinegar to onions and cook, stirring, for 3 minutes longer or until onions are golden.

Serves 8

Take care when cooking this dish, as once the honey is added the mixture will brown very quickly and can easily burn.

Rosemary Baked Potatoes

8 medium new potatoes
2 tablespoons vegetable oil
2 tablespoons fresh rosemary leaves
or 1 teaspoon dried rosemary
sea salt

1   Cut four sheets of foil each large enough to enclose four potatoes. Place two sheets on top of each other, then place four potatoes on each.

2   Brush potatoes with oil and sprinkle with rosemary and salt. Fold foil around potatoes to enclose. Roll edges together to seal well.

3   Place foil packages in the hot coals of the barbecue and cook, turning occasionally, for 35-45 minutes or until potatoes are tender.

Serves 8

If you have a gas barbecue, place the parcels on the side of the barbecue and cook, turning occasionally, for 1 hour or until the potatoes are tender.

Peach Cheesecake

PEACH CHEESECAKE

peach slices for garnish
passion fruit pulp for garnish

HAZELNUT BASE
125 g/4 oz plain sweet biscuit crumbs
170 g/5^1/$_2$ oz finely chopped
toasted hazelnuts
75 g/2^1/$_2$ oz butter, melted

PEACH FILLING
250 g/8 oz cream cheese, softened
^{1}/$_2$ cup/100 g/3^1/$_2$ oz caster sugar
4 peaches, peeled and chopped
300 mL/9^1/$_2$ oz cream (double)
4 teaspoons gelatine dissolved in 2
tablespoons boiling water, cooled
^{1}/$_3$ cup/90 mL/3 fl oz passion fruit pulp

1   To make base, place biscuit crumbs, hazelnuts and butter in a bowl and mix to combine. Press into base of a 20 cm/8 in springform tin. Refrigerate until firm.

2   To make filling, place cream cheese, sugar and peaches in a food processor or blender and process until smooth.

3   Transfer peach mixture to a bowl and whisk in cream. Stir gelatine mixture and passion fruit pulp into peach mixture.

4   Pour filling into prepared tin and refrigerate for 4 hours or until filling is set. Just prior to serving, decorate with peach slices and passion fruit pulp.

Serves 8

If fresh peaches are unavailable, drained canned peaches can be used instead.

Oriental Inspiration

Prawn and Wonton Soup

Ginger Chilli Crab

Sesame Beef with Snow Peas

Sautéed Chinese Greens

Fried Rice

Melon with Ginger Syrup

SERVES 6-8

Prawn and Wonton Soup

2¹/₂ litres/4 pt chicken stock
1 carrot, cut into thin strips
1 stalk celery, cut into thin strips
¹/₂ red pepper, cut into thin strips
24 large cooked prawns, shelled
and deveined

PORK WONTONS
250 g/8 oz pork mince
1 egg, lightly beaten
2 spring onions, chopped
1 fresh red chilli, seeded and chopped
1 tablespoon soy sauce
1 tablespoon oyster sauce
24 spring roll or wonton wrappers,
each 12.5 cm/5 in square

1   To make wontons, place pork, egg, spring onions, chilli, soy sauce and oyster sauce in a bowl and mix to combine.

2   Place spoonfuls of mixture in the centre of each spring roll or wonton wrapper, then draw the corners together and twist to form small bundles. Place wontons in a steamer set over a saucepan of boiling water and steam for 3-4 minutes or until wontons are cooked.

3   Place chicken stock in a saucepan and bring to the boil over a medium heat. Add carrot, celery and red pepper and simmer for 1 minute. Add prawns and cook for 1 minute longer.

4   To serve, place 3-4 wontons in each soup bowl and carefully ladle over soup. Serve immediately.

Serves 6-8

For even cooking, make sure that the wontons are not touching when you place them in the steamer.

Ginger Chilli Crab

1 tablespoon vegetable oil
2 cloves garlic, crushed
3 tablespoons desiccated coconut
2 tablespoons grated fresh ginger
¹/₂ cup/125 mL/4 fl oz sweet chilli sauce
6 spring onions, chopped
2 tablespoons fish sauce
4 uncooked crabs, cleaned and quartered
2 tablespoons chopped fresh coriander

1   Heat oil in a wok over a medium heat. Add garlic, coconut and ginger and stir-fry for 1 minute.

2   Stir in chilli sauce, spring onions and fish sauce and cook for 1 minute longer.

3   Add crab pieces and coriander and stir-fry for 3 minutes or until crab pieces change colour and are cooked.

Serves 6-8

If crab is unavailable, you could use large uncooked prawns for this recipe.

Prawn and Wonton Soup

SESAME BEEF WITH SNOW PEAS

1 kg/2 lb rump steak, trimmed of all
visible fat and cut into wide strips
$^1/_4$ cup/30 g/1 oz cornflour
2 teaspoons vegetable oil
1 teaspoon sesame oil
2 tablespoons soy sauce
2 tablespoons oyster sauce
2 tablespoons hoisin sauce
300 g/9$^1/_2$ oz snow peas (mangetout)
3 tablespoons sesame seeds, toasted

1   Toss steak in cornflour to coat, shake
off excess and set aside.

2   Heat a wok or large frying pan over a
high heat. Add vegetable and sesame oils
and steak and stir-fry for 2 minutes. Stir in
soy sauce, oyster sauce and hoisin sauce
and stir-fry for 1 minute longer.

3   Add snow peas (mangetout) and
sesame seeds and stir-fry for 1 minute or
until snow peas (mangetout) are just
cooked. Serve immediately.

Serves 6-8

As several of the dishes for
this menu require last-minute
cooking, it is important to do
as much as possible of the
preparation in advance.
Sauces can be mixed, meat
and fish cut up and
vegetables chopped.

SAUTEED CHINESE GREENS

300 g/9¹/₂ oz bok choy
300 g/9¹/₂ oz Chinese broccoli
300 g/9¹/₂ oz Chinese mustard cabbage
or Chinese cabbage
1 tablespoon vegetable oil
2 teaspoons black bean paste
2 cloves garlic, crushed
3 tablespoons oyster sauce
2 tablespoons water

The vegetables used in this recipe are available from Asian food shops, good greengrocers and some supermarkets.

1   Trim thick stalks from bok choy, broccoli and cabbage. Discard stalks and chop leaves into large pieces.

2   Heat wok or large frying pan over a medium heat. Add oil, black bean paste, garlic, oyster sauce and water and stir-fry for 2 minutes.

3   Add vegetables and stir-fry for 2 minutes or until leaves are wilted.

Serves 6-8

FRIED RICE

1 tablespoon vegetable oil
2 eggs, lightly beaten
6 spring onions, chopped
3 rashers bacon or 3 Chinese
sausages, chopped
1 red pepper, chopped
250 g/8 oz uncooked prawns,
shelled and deveined
90 g/3 oz canned or frozen
sweet corn kernels
500 g/1 lb long grain rice,
cooked and chilled
3 tablespoons soy sauce

Rice for fried rice should be cooked and refrigerated overnight before using. As the rice cools, the grains dry out and this prevents the fried rice from being sticky.

1   Heat 2 teaspoons oil in a wok or large frying pan over a medium heat. Add eggs and swirl pan so eggs form a thin omelette. Cook for 1 minute, turn and cook for 1 minute longer. Remove omelette from pan, roll and cut into thin slices. Set aside.

2   Heat remaining oil in clean wok or frying pan over a high heat. Add spring onions, bacon or sausages, red pepper and prawns and stir-fry for 3 minutes or until prawns change colour.

3   Add sweet corn, rice and soy sauce to pan and stir-fry for 2 minutes. Add egg strips and stir-fry for 1 minute longer.

Serves 6-8

Melon with Ginger Syrup

MELON WITH GINGER SYRUP

400 g/12¹/₂ oz watermelon,
cut into thick strips
300 g/9¹/₂ oz honeydew melon,
cut into thick strips
300 g/9¹/₂ oz rock melon (cantaloupe),
cut into thick strips

GINGER SYRUP
45 g/1¹/₂ oz preserved ginger in syrup,
thinly sliced
1 cup/250 mL/8 fl oz sweet ginger wine
2 tablespoons sugar
1 tablespoon thin lemon rind strips

1   Arrange watermelon, honeydew melon and rock melon (cantaloupe) on a serving platter. Cover and chill until required.

2   To make Ginger Syrup, place ginger, wine, sugar and lemon strips in a saucepan, bring to simmering over a medium heat and simmer, stirring occasionally, for 3 minutes. Transfer syrup to a bowl, cover and chill.

3   Just prior to serving, spoon syrup over melon.

Serves 6-8

Use any combination of melons that are available for this recipe.

More Dash than Cash

Bruschetta with Tomato and Basil

Bruschetta with Eggplant and Feta

Sweet Potato and Leek Soup

Vineyard Chicken

Crunchy Green Beans

Steamed Rice or Crusty Bread

Pear Tarts with Maple Cream

SERVES 4-6

BRUSCHETTA

1 French bread stick, cut into
1 cm/^{1}/2 in slices
2 tablespoons olive oil
2 cloves garlic, halved

TOMATO AND BASIL TOPPING
2 tomatoes, sliced
1 red onion, sliced
2 tablespoons shredded basil leaves

EGGPLANT AND FETA TOPPING
2 baby eggplant (aubergines), sliced
1 tablespoon olive oil
125 g/4 oz feta cheese, crumbled
freshly ground black pepper

1   Brush bread slices with oil, place under a preheated hot grill and toast both sides until golden. Rub one side of toasts with cut side of garlic cloves.

2   For Tomato and Basil Topping, top half the toast slices with some tomato, onion and basil, and grill for 1-2 minutes or until topping is warm.

3   For Eggplant and Feta Topping, brush eggplant (aubergine) slices with oil and cook under preheated hot grill for 3-4 minutes each side or until lightly browned. Top remaining toasts with eggplant (aubergine) slices and sprinkle with feta cheese and black pepper to taste. Cook under a preheated hot grill for 1-2 minutes or until topping is warm.

Bruschetta

Makes 16-20

Sweet Potato and Leek Soup

Sweet Potato and Leek Soup

1 kg/2 lb orange sweet potatoes,
cut into large pieces
2 onions, halved
2 leeks, halved
4 cups/1 litre/1³/4 pt chicken stock
2 cups/500 mL/16 fl oz water
1 teaspoon ground cumin
freshly ground black pepper
sour cream to garnish
fresh mint to garnish

1 Place sweet potatoes, onions and leeks in a well-greased baking dish and bake for 45 minutes or until vegetables are tender. Remove from oven and set aside to cool slightly.

2 Place baked vegetables, stock, water, cumin and black pepper to taste, in batches, in a food processor or blender and process until smooth.

3 Place soup into a large saucepan, bring to simmering over a medium heat and simmer, stirring occasionally, for 3-4 minutes or until soup is hot.

4 To serve, ladle soup into bowls, and garnish with a spoonful of sour cream and fresh mint. Serve immediately.

Serves 4-6

Oven temperature
200°C, 400°F, Gas 6

This soup can be made the day before and reheated when required.

75

VINEYARD CHICKEN

4 boneless chicken breast or thigh fillets
2 teaspoons vegetable oil
2 onions, sliced
2 cloves garlic, crushed
440 g/14 oz canned tomatoes,
undrained and mashed
1 green pepper, chopped
1 cup/250 mL/4 fl oz dry white wine

RICOTTA FILLING
125 g/4 oz ricotta cheese, drained
2 tablespoons chopped fresh basil
freshly ground black pepper

To serve six, increase the
ingredients by half.
This recipe can be
completed to the end of
step 2 several hours in
advance.

1 Make a deep slit in the side of each
chicken fillet to form a pocket.

2 To make filling, place ricotta cheese,
basil and black pepper to taste in a bowl
and mix to combine. Fill pocket in fillets
with filling and secure with toothpicks.

3 Heat oil in a large frying pan, add
onions and garlic and cook, stirring, for 3
minutes or until onions are soft. Add
tomatoes, green pepper and wine to pan
and cook, stirring, for 2 minutes.

4 Add chicken to pan, cover and
simmer, turning chicken occasionally, for
30 minutes or until chicken is tender.

Serves 4

CRUNCHY GREEN BEANS

375 g/12 oz green beans
30 g/1 oz tablespoons butter, melted
3 tablespoons chopped hazelnuts
1/2 cup/30 g/1 oz breadcrumbs, made
from stale bread
2 spring onions, finely chopped

This is also a delicious way to
cook carrots. Cut them into
strips, lengthwise, and cook
as described in this recipe.

1 Boil, steam or microwave beans until
just tender. Drain, refresh under running
cold water and drain well.

2 Melt butter in a frying pan over a
medium heat. Add hazelnuts,
breadcrumbs, spring onions and beans
and cook, stirring, for 2 minutes or until
breadcrumb mixture is golden. Serve
immediately.

Serves 4-6

Vineyard Chicken, Crunchy Green Beans

PEAR TARTS WITH MAPLE CREAM

155 g/5 oz prepared puff pastry
2 pears, cored, peeled and halved,
stems left intact
2 cups/500 mL/16 fl oz water
1 cup/250 g/8 oz sugar
2 cloves
1 cinnamon stick
1 egg yolk, lightly beaten
1 tablespoon brown sugar

MAPLE CREAM
2 tablespoons icing sugar
1 cup/200 g/6^1/$_2$ oz vanilla yogurt
3 tablespoons maple syrup

1   Roll out pastry to 5 mm/^{1}/$_4$ in thick and, using a pear half as a guide, cut pastry into four pear shapes, each 2 cm/^{3}/$_4$ in larger than a pear half.

2   Place water, sugar, cloves, cinnamon stick and pears in a saucepan and bring to simmering over a medium heat. Simmer for 4 minutes or until pears are half cooked. Remove pears from syrup and drain well.

3   Brush pastry shapes with egg yolk, top each with a pear half and sprinkle with brown sugar. Place on a baking tray and bake for 15 minutes or until pastry is puffed and golden and pears are tender.

4   To make Maple Cream, place icing sugar, yogurt and maple syrup in a bowl and beat until smooth. Serve with tarts.

Serves 4

Oven temperature
180°C, 350°F, Gas 4

To serve six, increase the ingredients by half.
This recipe can be completed to the end of step 2 several hours in advance.

INDEX

UK COOKERY EDITOR
Katie Swallow

EDITORIAL
Food Editor: Rachel Blackmore
Editorial and Production Assistant: Sheridan Packer
Assistant Editor: Ella Martin
Editorial Coordinator: Margaret Kelly

Photography: Quentin Bacon

Food and Styling: Donna Hay
Home Economist: Jodie Vassallo

DESIGN AND PRODUCTION
Manager: Sheridan Carter
Layout and Design: Lulu Dougherty
Cover Design: Frank Pithers

Published by J.B. Fairfax Press Pty Limited
80-82 McLachlan Avenue
Rushcutters Bay 2011
A.C.N. 003 738 430

Formatted by J.B. Fairfax Press Pty Limited
Printed by Toppan Printing Co, Hong Kong

JBFP 299 UK
Includes Index
ISBN 1 86343 138 1

Distributed by J. B. Fairfax Press Ltd
9 Trinity Centre, Park Farm Estate
Wellingborough, Northants
Ph: (0933) 402330 Fax: (0933) 402234

Marketing in the Era of Accountability

Identifying the marketing practices and
metrics that truly increase profitability

Les Binet, DDB Matrix
Peter Field, Marketing Consultant

Published by Warc

First published June 2007 by Warc
Reprinted August 2007, February 2008, March 2008 (with revisions) and October 2010

Warc Ltd
85 Newman Street, London, W1T 3EX, UK
Telephone: +44 (0)20 7467 8100
Facsimile: +44 (0)20 7467 8101
Email: info@warc.com
www.warc.com

A CIP catalogue record for this book is
available from the British Library

ISBN 978-1-84116-198-3

Printed and bound in Great Britain by Marston Book Services Limited

Contents

Editorial Advisory Board

The IPA dataMINE project is guided by:

Les Binet
European Director
DDB Matrix

Hugh Burkitt
CEO
The Marketing Society

Gerard Chick
Head of Knowledge Management
Chartered Institute of Purchasing & Supply

Matthew Coombs
Publishing Director
WARC

Laurence Green
Founding Partner
Fallon London

Janet Hull
Head of Marketing and Reputation Management
Institute of Practitioners in Advertising

Roderick White
Editor
Admap

The IPA dataMINE project

Writing in 1980, in the preface to the first edition of *Advertising Works*, Simon Broadbent set out the three key aims of the IPA Effectiveness Awards:

- A better understanding of the crucial role advertising plays in marketing.
- Closer analysis of advertising effectiveness and improved methods of evaluation.
- A clear demonstration that advertising can be proven to work, against measurable criteria.

Over 25 years and over 1000 papers later, the IPA Effectiveness Awards have grown in scale and stature, and become the international gold standard of advertising case material. These days, entering and winning the IPA Awards is a public demonstration of agency commitment to accountability.

The IPA online dataBANK search facility allows learning from the complete set of cases to be quantified for the first time, in order to produce normative data on advertising-related topics. Quantitative findings can then be illustrated, or supplemented, by individual case examples.

The IPA dataMINE series seeks to build on this impressive body of evidence. It supports the IPA's aim to better promote the perceived and real value of IPA member agencies to client business, to opinion formers in business, government and the City. Designed to fuse theory and practice, contributors are invited to challenge the database of IPA cases to prove or disprove pet theories; to look for patterns; arrive at principles; test intuition; hone thinking and share knowledge.

This issue, the second in our series, is the result of 18 months' hard work and analysis. It marks an important milestone in advertising knowledge. We are indebted to Les Binet and Peter Field for producing this 'magnum opus', for their dedication and their commitment to leaving no stone unturned in their process of interrogation. We are also grateful to DDB, an agency that has contributed more cases to the dataBANK over the years than any other, for allowing Les Binet and Alex Vass to work on the project.

JANET HULL
Head of Marketing and Reputation Management
Institute of Practitioners in Advertising

Acknowledgements

The authors would like to acknowledge the help and input of the following in putting this publication together:

Tim Ambler, Matthew Coombs, Paul Feldwick, Janet Hull and Roderick White for having the patience to read the draft and for providing many helpful comments to improve it.

Martin Deboo for his invaluable input into measures of financial return.

Simon Thompson for his stimulating observations on brand metrics used whilst Marketing Director of Honda UK.

Alex Vass for the many hours he spent helping to produce and present the data.

Caroline Roberts for helping to source many of the references.

Jill Bentley for her unerring eye for detail in seeing the project through to print.

And finally the late lamented Simon Broadbent, without whose foresight none of this analysis would have been possible.

Foreword

Demand generation is arguably the most important business function in today's hyper-competitive environment, and effective marketing communications are the prime means of doing this for many companies.

However, it is very hard to answer some of the basic questions – what business goals make the best objectives? Do rational or emotional communications work best? Should the focus be on deepening loyalty or widening penetration? Is TV advertising less effective in today's media environment? The list goes on, and there is a clear need for real-world proofs and 'rules-of-thumb' to help decision making, rather than relying on theory or subjective judgement.

Generating rigorous case studies to prove the effectiveness of communications has been the role of the IPA Effectiveness Awards since 1980, and the body of data within these cases is arguably the most comprehensive and robust in existence.

Les Binet and Peter Field have a deep understanding of the IPA case study dataBANK, having both been centrally involved in setting it up. In this impressive publication they show how the accumulated learning from the cases can be applied to everyday practice. It is an invaluable summary of general proofs and 'lessons', and highlights the critical success factors (and also what, by comparison, works less well) for highly effective communications. The report contains important findings which will resonate in boardrooms everywhere.

We are proud that DDB staff helped create this report, as effectiveness is deeply ingrained in our culture. Stanley Pollitt, the originator of the planning discipline in our agency (and in the UK advertising industry), always strived to put hard-nosed business success at the heart of any evaluation of communications. As this publication demonstrates, the distilled learning from past success can provide us with valuable lessons to improve the effectiveness of communications in the future.

STEPHEN WOODFORD
Chairman and Chief Executive Officer
DDB London

Executive summary

The IPA Effectiveness Awards are well known for being the world's most rigorous effectiveness awards scheme. What is less well known is that the competition has enabled the IPA to build up a huge database of confidential information on the factors that make marketing work. This publication outlines an analysis of that data. Based on a sample of 880 case studies, it is probably the largest meta-analysis of its kind ever undertaken. It not only reveals some of the factors that make marketing profitable, but also exposes some common practices and beliefs that lead to waste and inefficiency. In particular:

- Contrary to received wisdom, focusing on a single campaign objective does not make marketing more effective. Objectives should be detailed and above all *prioritised*.

- Marketers pay too much attention to intermediate attitudinal measures, and too little to business and behavioural outcomes. Although brand health (sometimes referred to as 'brand equity') is an important stepping-stone to business success, it is not an end in itself.

- When marketers do focus on business measures, they focus on the wrong ones: sales rather than market share, and volume rather than value.

- Marketers focus on the wrong behavioural outcomes too. Most campaigns aim to increase loyalty, but increasing penetration is far more effective and profitable.

- The drive for accountability leads marketers to focus on a narrow range of intermediate key performance indicators (KPIs), particularly awareness and direct responses. However, there is no single measure that reliably predicts effectiveness, and focusing on individual metrics actually *reduces* effectiveness.

- This raises questions about the reliability of pre-testing. The data suggest that pre-testing may even *reduce* effectiveness.

- A 'balanced scorecard' approach to measuring brand health leads to better results. If a single KPI is required, it should be a 'metric of metrics'.

- The need for accountability often makes marketers focus on rational product messages. In fact, emotional campaigns are more powerful, even in 'rational' categories.

- Of the emotional approaches, the 'fame' model turns out to be particularly powerful. Yet marketers tend to neglect fame in favour of more limited goals.

- Marketers often focus on absolute levels of spend or advertising-to-sales ratios when setting budgets. In fact, share of voice is a better KPI. This report outlines a detailed method for setting budgets based on this measure.

- There is little evidence to support the widespread assumption that TV is becoming less effective. In fact, TV effectiveness may be *increasing*.

- On the other hand, the fashion for 'surround sound' in media may be less than ideal. Integration is good, but more channels is not always better.

- Marketing needs to focus more on profit and less on return on investment (ROI). Much talk of ROI is confused, and some of it leads to poor business decisions. The use of ROI as a ratio can be dangerous in the marketing context and so a better alternative is proposed here.

- Econometrics is much less common than it should be. Used properly, it can improve accountability *and* effectiveness.

Many of these problems can be traced back to a tension between *effectiveness* (doing the right thing) and *accountability* (being seen to do the right thing). This publication investigates this conflict and attempts to reconcile it by making specific recommendations for best practice in marketing.

1 Introduction

Aims

This publication is about the pursuit of profitability, not the winning of prizes. It aims chiefly to narrow the gap between common practice and best practice in marketing, by identifying key drivers of effective marketing – effective in terms of maximising payback. It is clear when it comes to marketing metrics and practices that *all that glisters is not gold*: the pressures of accountability that increasingly shape marketing do not always lead to improved business results. So this publication will separate out the misleadingly glittering from the truly golden.

Although much of the data examined relate principally to communications, they also record a wide range of success factors that shed useful light on broader aspects of marketing effectiveness. They will draw chiefly on the IPA dataBANK of effectiveness case studies – not in an anecdotal, *qualitative* sense (as is usually the case), quoting cases selectively that fit an argument, but *quantitatively*, drawing robust conclusions from the body of cases. Throughout, the objective will be to extract the lessons for the future from the case studies. Where relevant, findings are used to validate authoritative academic and consultancy research.

As part of providing guidance on how to maximise the effectiveness of marketing, this publication also aims to inform the choice of metrics used to monitor marketing. In particular, this has strong implications for the design of value-based remuneration schemes for agencies. If value-based remuneration is to successfully drive effectiveness then it must be based on sound measurement of effectiveness and on its key drivers.

The IPA Effectiveness Awards

The late Simon Broadbent established the IPA Effectiveness Awards scheme in 1980 to encourage a focus on effectiveness among UK advertising agencies and to raise standards of evaluation and proof. It has become the world's most rigorous competition of effectiveness case studies. Unlike many other effectiveness competitions, judgment is based solely on business success and on the quality of the proof that is provided. To this end, the evidence is double-vetted by industry experts plus senior clients and academics. The evidence (in the shape of the written case studies) is published and open to public scrutiny: any of the case studies referred to in this publication can be downloaded from the WARC website.

The judging panel of senior business people, academics and researchers only awards prizes to case studies that prove effectiveness beyond reasonable doubt.

The IPA dataBANK

The IPA dataBANK is the product of the Awards: case studies codified in a standard format. It is best understood as a large spreadsheet of over 880 national case studies, each classified by a number of defining characteristics covering over 30 topics. In all, 216 fields record the nature of the brands and of the campaigns, their circumstances and, crucially, their results.

Up to 1996, the coding was undertaken by expert reviewers of the papers and is therefore limited to the areas covered in the written paper. However, since 1998 the standardised data have been captured by a compulsory (but confidential) questionnaire submitted by Awards entrants, in addition to the written paper. The questionnaire is available in the Appendix to this publication. Gaps in the data have, as a result, been dramatically reduced. The analyses reported in this publication are therefore chiefly based on cases submitted since 1998, because more data is available from then on. These data therefore also include a lot of information not reported in the written papers, but which adds hugely to their value. The number of cases reporting data for each of the topics is shown in Table 1.

Table 1: The volume of data by topic

Topic	Number of cases reporting data	Topic	Number of cases reporting data
ANY–ALL NATIONAL CASES	880	Creative style of TV advertising	422
Brand size	416	Communications influence model	410
Price position	383	Impact measures used	630
Business objectives	839	Standout measures used	405
Nature of marketing initiative	766	Brand perception measures used	715
Communications goals	435	Behavioural measures used	419
Target market	844	Intermediate consumer effects	382
Product category	367	Market measures used	821
Category life stage	417	Business effects	586
Category growth	386	Market share by volume	171
Role of rational consideration in choice	377	Market share by value	155
Role of emotional consideration in choice	359	Longer and broader effects	369
Media/channels used	456	Return on investment	203
Marketing budget	232	Collateral effects	321
Lead medium/channel	338	Method of proof of causality	659
Number of media	430	Other awards	721
UK/regional/international	845	Details of any IPA prizes awarded	880
Share of voice	222		

There are also a number of regional UK case studies available in the dataBANK that would bring the total to over 1200, but these are not analysed in this publication for two reasons: the level of reporting and proof was lower and the most successful regional case studies often go on to enter the national Awards and so would be 'double counted'.

The IPA dataBANK is a unique body of objective, comparable data that observes the conditions of proven effective campaigns. It is clearly not a random sample of campaigns, but rather a selection of examples of best practice in effectiveness. The campaigns themselves are increasingly integrated campaigns: the products of agencies from different communications channels working to common brand briefs. The dataBANK thus represents the most complete, objective UK record and definition of effectiveness today and arguably the leading such resource anywhere in the world.

Methodology

The data offer five main measures that can be used to examine effectiveness and accountability. These are listed below in Table 2, along with the number of cases that report each measure. The analysis takes account of any gaps in the data by excluding a case study if the data for the fields involved are incomplete. For this reason the base for each analysis varies and is seldom all 880 papers.

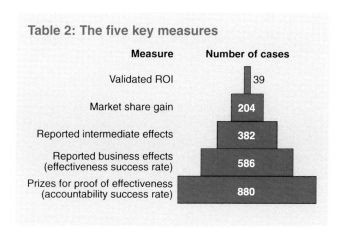

Table 2: The five key measures

Of these five measures two are especially important to this publication. These are the 'effectiveness success rate' and the 'accountability success rate'. They are explained below in the 'Claimed business effects' and 'Prizes for proof of effectiveness' sections.

As has been noted, earlier cases are more commonly excluded from analyses because their data are more often incomplete, but where they are able to be included the data are reliable. The nature and usage of the five measures are outlined below.

Return on investment (ROI)

The quantity of payback data is limited (often for reasons of confidentiality) and is usually flawed (see Part 7). So all cases reporting payback data were examined in detail and only where the data were found to be reliable were they included in the analysis. This left 39 cases with validated payback data. So, although this is arguably the ultimate measure of effectiveness, it is too limited in availability to use directly. Instead, it is used to validate the proxy measure of effectiveness (see 'Claimed business effects' on page 14).

Market share gain

Although market share is not necessarily the only driver of profitability, PIMS data (Buzzell & Gale, 1987) demonstrate that it is a primary factor in profitability (see page 25 for more information on PIMS). However, the quantity of market share growth data is too limited for statistically reliable fine breakdowns. So the measure is used where feasible for broad analyses and, in particular, for examination of the impact of share of voice on growth. Wherever possible value share gain is the preferred measure, but volume share is used when it is not available.

Claimed intermediate effects

Intermediate effects refer to *consumer* measures such as brand awareness, image and other measures of consumer 'brand health'. Some people refer to these measures as 'brand equity', but that is not a term that will be used in this publication because of its ambiguity (see Part 2). The volume of data here is useful, but as will be shown, intermediate effects do not reliably correlate with business performance. Clearly, marketing can only improve business performance if it changes the pattern of thoughts, feelings, associations and habits evoked by a brand (even if consumers are not always aware of such changes). But the evidence of the dataBANK is that there does not yet appear to be widespread reliable measurement of intermediate effects in a way that can predict subsequent behaviour and business effects. So the data are primarily used to examine *how* communications work rather than whether they do. Nevertheless, a way of using intermediate data is reported that improves its predictive capability of business results, and this is proposed as an approach for a *leading* indicator of business effectiveness.

Claimed business effects

The business effects data include a wide-ranging assessment of the changes that resulted from the campaign that can be used to examine the impact of market factors as well as marketing practices. These assessments include sales and share gains, price sensitivity, customer loyalty, penetration and, of course, profit. The scale of a business effect is assessed by the case study author (in the compulsory questionnaire) as being 'very large', 'large/substantial' or 'small/negligible'. The relevant question from the authors' questionnaire is reproduced below.

Throughout this publication the chosen measure of success of a particular practice is the proportion of those cases that reported any '*very large*' business effects: this is referred to as the 'Effectiveness Success Rate'.

Assessment of the scale of business effect in the authors' questionnaire

Q28: Please assess the scale of changes to each of the following measures over the course of the evaluation period (please use your own subjective judgment based on your experience of advertising in the market)

	Very large	Large/ substantial	Small/ negligible
Sales gain	❏	❏	❏
Market share gain	❏	❏	❏
Reduction of price sensitivity	❏	❏	❏
Customer retention/loyalty increase	❏	❏	❏
New customer acquisition/penetration	❏	❏	❏
Profit gain	❏	❏	❏
Other (please specify)	❏	❏	❏

The assessment is clearly subjective to a degree, but it does have the advantage of being related to the circumstances of the brand and norms of the category. It yields a very significant body of data (586 cases) that permits detailed analysis of what works – that is, which measures and characteristics of campaigns are most closely associated with success in various circumstances. From this, conclusions can be drawn about the key drivers of *effectiveness*.

It should be noted that because the dataBANK is a collection of successful case studies, the effectiveness success rates are generally high. What is important is not their absolute level, but the relative levels achieved by different practices and whether they are above average or not (i.e. do they appear to promote success or reduce it). In this way, any biases due to the nature of the sample (all cases are competitors in an effectiveness competition) can be eliminated.

The reasons for using the compound measure of business success rather than a straightforward measure of profit growth have already been stated: principally, that the reporting of actual profit growth is restricted to a small number of cases that is insufficient to support the depth of analysis that is reported here. So the effectiveness success rate has been developed as a proxy for profit growth. The extent to which this is a good proxy for profit growth is explored below.

The effectiveness success rate is a good proxy for profit growth
The reliability of this proxy measure can be tested by comparing it to the 39 reliable measures of actual ROI that we do have. Since the effectiveness success rate is defined as the proportion of cases reporting any very large business effects, one would expect to observe higher ROIs for such cases if the measure is a good proxy for profitability. This is indeed the case, confirming the broad validity of the proxy measure (see Table 3).

Table 3: Relationship between claimed business effects and actual ROI		
	Campaigns reporting any very large business effects	**Campaigns not reporting very large business effects**
Average ROI reported	620%	390%

What is more, cases reporting larger ROIs were more likely to report 'very large' business effects rather than 'large' or 'small' ones, whereas cases reporting smaller ROIs were more likely to report lesser business effects (see Appendix).

So it can generally be assumed that the observations and recommendations made in relation to increasing the effectiveness success rate are likely to hold true for improving ROI.

The proxy measure holds good as a predictor of market share gains too (see Figure 1).

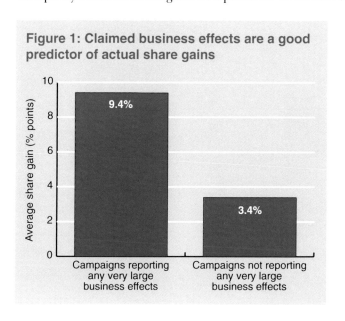

Figure 1: Claimed business effects are a good predictor of actual share gains

In addition, the more very large business effects observed, the greater the share gain (see Figure 2).

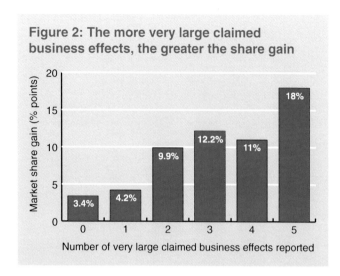

Figure 2: The more very large claimed business effects, the greater the share gain

The correlation between the number of very large business effects and the gain of market share is very strong: it is significant at the 99% confidence level. The effectiveness success rate is therefore the key measure of effectiveness used in this publication.

Prizes for proof of effectiveness

Throughout this publication the chosen measure of accountability of a particular practice is the proportion of those cases that won prizes in the Awards: this is referred to as the 'Accountability Success Rate'. This measure includes the largest possible volume of data. The dataBANK includes prize-winning and non prize-winning cases. The prize data are not used as a measure of effectiveness because they are principally a measure of level of proof, not scale of business success: that is, how convincing was the case that the campaign had been effective? So, because the prizes awarded by judges (many of whom are senior managers of major advertisers) are a measure of what evidence convinced them most, comparisons between winners and non-winners can yield conclusions about which KPIs are best for demonstrating *accountability*. In general, effectiveness and accountability tend to go together. However, this is not always the case as will be shown.

Significance testing

All the data reported in this publication have been significance tested and the notation shown in Table 4 indicates the level of significance attached to each result (the absence of any notation means the result is not significant at the 90% level).

Table 4: Significance notation

Confidence level	Results above average	Results below average
90%	(+)	(–)
95%	(++)	(– –)
99%	(+++)	(– – –)

So if data were reported thus: 78% (++), it would mean that the value 78% was greater than the average a campaign could expect and that this was significant at the 95% confidence level.

Reasons for this analytical approach

There are a number of potential concerns that might be raised about the use of the dataBANK as a source for drawing conclusions about key drivers of effective marketing. These are listed below, along with the means by which the analytical approach taken in this publication overcomes them:

1. *'This is not a random sample of campaigns – these are much more successful than an average campaign'*
   The analysis therefore compares the best with the good to draw conclusions about best practice.

2. *'Authors tend to exaggerate to win prizes'*
   This analysis assumes that they all do, and therefore:

   - to gauge effects uses objective data from the questionnaire, which is independent of the written competition papers
   - focuses on cases showing only the very largest claimed effects to identify best practice.

3. *'Judges are influenced by factors other than hard measures of success'*
   Therefore prizes awarded are used only to assess the level of accountability achieved. Effectiveness is assessed by more objective measures.

4. *'Are there enough data on non-TV channels?'*
   In fact, there is sufficient channel diversity amongst the case studies to enable robust examination of many non-advertising channels and non-TV campaigns. Table 5 reveals the diversity of channels covered by the dataBANK.

Table 5: The diversity of channel usage among case studies

Media/channels used	Number of cases
TV	389
Press	291
Posters	188
Radio	146
Internet	104
PR	95
Direct marketing	89
Sales promotions	87
Couponing	45
Cinema	41
Sponsorship	28
Other	81

5. *'Are there enough data on categories other than fast-moving consumer goods?'*
   Again there is sufficient diversity to enable robust examination of other categories, as Table 6 evidences.

Table 6: Categories examined by case studies	
Category	Number of cases
fmcg	476
Durables	104
Services	202
Not-for-profit	98

6. *'Are the data exclusively UK based?'*

This concern is largely true, although there are 23 case studies that are either wholly non-UK or at least international in scope. However, it seems likely that the conclusions drawn are broadly applicable to other developed economies.

Structure of this publication

The order in which the many factors that shape effective marketing are examined in this publication is not intended to reflect their relative importance. Rather, they are discussed in the order in which they typically arise during the planning cycle of a campaign.

Part 2 looks at how to brief a campaign, and what goals and targets need to be set to ensure that the campaign is both effective and accountable.

Part 3 then looks at how to set budgets, and suggests a method that should improve the chances of meeting those campaign objectives.

Having set the budget, Part 4 looks at campaign strategy, and identifies the ingredients that do (and don't) seem to affect how effectively that budget is deployed.

Meanwhile, Part 5 looks at effectiveness from the perspective of media strategy.

Having set targets and budgets, and decided on strategies for both media and message, Part 6 looks at the tricky question of measurement, both before and after the campaign runs. Which measurement techniques make a campaign more accountable? And which best promote effectiveness? As will be shown, these two things are not always the same. This leads naturally to the question of payback.

Part 7 looks at how to measure payback in financial terms, and what factors seem to lead to the high returns. Part 7 concludes with a discussion of the thorny issue of payment by results.

Each section is further broken down into key topics, each sub-headed. Unless otherwise stated, all data quoted in this publication are derived from the IPA dataBANK. Further details concerning the data can be found in the Appendix.

2 Briefing

This part will examine the nature and pattern of objectives that should be set for marketing and communications if effectiveness is to be maximised. This should constitute a coherent 'roadmap' of business, brand and communications objectives; no campaign should be developed without this clear statement of objectives and the corresponding measures of success.

General approach

Set clear objectives

Marketing is unlikely to be effective, and certainly success will be difficult to measure, if objectives are not clearly spelled out. This is largely a consequence of the very definition of 'effectiveness' – best laid down by Tim Ambler as 'reaching desired goals' (Ambler 1999). Agreeing clear objectives makes marketing more accountable because it provides definite criteria for judging success or failure. Less obviously, agreeing clear objectives also makes marketing more effective, by focusing minds and resources on the tasks that matter. Evidence from the dataBANK suggests that **campaigns that set clear campaign objectives are more effective than those that don't** (see Figure 3).

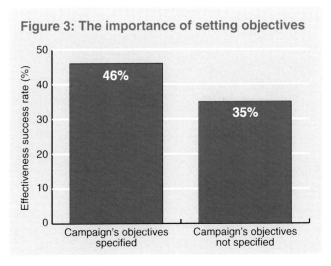

Figure 3: The importance of setting objectives

The more specific the objectives are, the more accountable the campaign will be. Ideally, objectives should be quantified, with intended timescales attached. However, it is clear (from the questionnaire responses) that even the brands featured in the dataBANK case studies rarely set precise business targets for their communications (though intermediate campaign response targets, such as awareness, are more frequently identified as KPIs); it is a safe assumption that quantified business targets are even rarer in the marketing world at large. Objectives may be identified, but are seldom quantified.

Focus on the objectives that matter

Setting clear objectives makes the communication process not only more accountable, but also more effective. However, not all kinds of objectives contribute equally to effectiveness and accountability.

Objectives can be divided into two types: hard and intermediate. Hard metrics measure factors that directly shape business performance – that is, business measures such as market share or pricing, or consumer behaviour measures such as penetration or loyalty. Thus, hard objectives can be further divided into two types: those that reflect *behavioural* changes by consumers and those that reflect the net *business* effects of these.

Intermediate metrics measure factors that will hopefully influence subsequent business performance, but do not directly affect the commercial position of the brand. They include non-financial measures of the *health* of the brand in the minds of consumers. As mentioned in the Introduction, these measures are sometimes referred to as 'brand equity' but they will be collectively referred to as 'brand health' in this publication for reasons outlined below. They are measures such as consumer awareness, attitudes and brand image. Intermediate metrics are seductive and widely used because they tend to move more quickly and impressively, and are easier to link to marketing activity. They are therefore useful (if used wisely) as leading indicators.

Why the term 'brand equity' is not used here

As Feldwick (2002) has observed, the term 'brand equity' is a very imprecise conflation of three concepts: brand valuation, brand appeal, and brand image. The term appears to have been invented in the 1980s to imbue intermediate brand attributes with financial associations. Arguably this is unjustified, unwise and unlikely to impress anyone from a financial background. It is currently often used loosely to include many different measures, whether or not they are likely to lead to business success.

The term 'brand health' is preferred here and refers to intermediate measures of brand perception by consumers that exert some influence over future business success. The validity of various components of brand health is discussed in this section and Part 6.

A clear finding from the dataBANK is that campaigns that are set hard objectives (business or behavioural results) are generally more successful than those working only to intermediate consumer response targets (e.g. attitudes or awareness). There are many factors at play that might account for this (discussed in later sections), but the general conclusion is that **marketing metrics should aim to measure changes in the real commercial world of the brand, not just the in the mindsets of the people who buy it.** This is true of not-for-profit brands as well (see Figure 4).

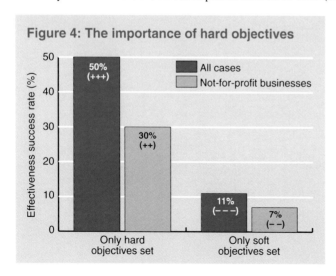

Figure 4: The importance of hard objectives

It is therefore axiomatic that **all briefs to communications agencies should include hard objectives** against which the success of the communications will be evaluated.

As a general conclusion, the dataBANK suggests that hard *business* objectives should take primacy over hard *behavioural* objectives, since the latter are more concerned with the 'how' than the 'what'. The overall hierarchy of objectives should therefore be:

1. Business objectives.
2. Behavioural objectives.
3. Intermediate objectives.

(For example, profit growth from greater consumer penetration from greater brand authority in the minds of consumers.)

More objectives are better

The evidence of the dataBANK (see Table 7) is that the benefit is greater the more hard objectives there are (within reason). In practice, on average, effective campaigns have two or three hard objectives, but would clearly often benefit from more.

Table 7: The benefit of more numerous hard objectives

	Number of hard objectives set		
	1	2–3	4+
Effectiveness success rate (% reporting very large business effects)	28% (– – –)	46%	76% (+++)
Accountability success rate (% winning awards)	41%	43%	66% (+++)

Taking prize winning as evidence of accountability, the dataBANK also suggests that multiple hard objectives make a campaign more accountable, perhaps because there are more measures of success or failure.

Views from the IPA Best Practice Guide 'Evaluation'

'Profitable growth from the strengthening of brand franchises and customer bases is what all advertisers are looking for when they invest in communications. It is the only reason for investing and the more accurately a company is able to quantify relevant 'effects' the easier it is to justify future expenditure internally.'

Malcolm Earnshaw
ISBA Director General

'What is evaluated should also be linked as closely as possible to the objectives of the business so that results have relevance, meaning and usefulness beyond the people working in PR.'

Steve Sargent
BT Marketing Services Purchasing Manager

Furthermore, the data show that it is more beneficial to have multiple hard business objectives if these are prioritised (see Figure 5). **Campaigns are significantly more likely to be successful if they define a hierarchy of objectives** (e.g. to increase profit by increasing market share by increasing penetration). However, only 15% of dataBANK cases did this, and it is a safe assumption that it is even less likely to be done in general practice.

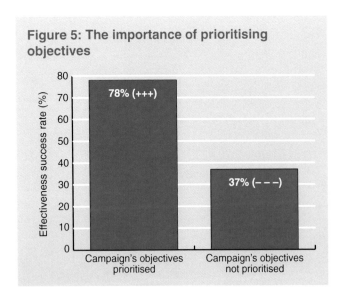

Figure 5: The importance of prioritising objectives

Business objectives

This section will examine the link between various business objectives and business success and accountability, in order to arrive at recommendations for business KPIs.

Make profit the ultimate objective

If successful campaigns tend to set objectives in terms of hard business measures, can the data suggest which business objectives are most appropriate? Table 8 reports the incidence of different business objectives and compares their success rates. Two things are immediately obvious from the table.

Table 8: Incidence and success rates of business objectives

	Campaign objective				
	Profit gain	Market share gain	Market share defence	Price sensitivity	Sales gain
Incidence among all cases	7%	25%	21%	4%	62%
Effectiveness success rate	84% (+++)	78% (+++)	52% (– –)	83% (+++)	51% (– – –)
Accountability success rate	77% (+++)	72% (+++)	59% (++)	63% (+)	41% (– – –)

First, **there is a wide mismatch between the incidence of objectives and their likelihood to lead to effectiveness** (very large effects) and accountability (winning awards). The least successful are often the most widely used, and vice versa. This issue will be revisited later.

Second, it is clear that **campaigns that aim to increase profitability outperform all others**, both in terms of effectiveness and accountability. Campaigns that make profit the *primary* objective do even better, with 92% reporting very large effects vs 84% of those that make profit just an objective (i.e. a primary or secondary objective).

The dataBANK can look deeper at the different kinds of effects different campaigns have. Looking at Table 9, which compares the performance of profit-focused campaigns (right-hand column) with all campaigns, it is clear that **profit-focused campaigns outperform others on every single business metric**. Of all the business objectives recorded, it has the highest success rate measured by the overall number of very large business effects it leads to.

Table 9: The greater effectiveness of profit-targeted campaigns

% reporting very large effects on:	Average of all campaigns disclosing hard objectives	Campaigns aiming to increase profit
Sales	45%	64% (+++)
Market share	25%	33% (+)
Profit	23%	54% (+++)
Penetration	23%	28%
Loyalty	7%	11% (+)
Price sensitivity	4%	13% (+++)
Any measure	**55%**	**84% (+++)**

So the finding is clear: **in the case of for-profit businesses, profit as a primary campaign objective strongly promotes success. All other objectives should be subservient to that end.**

Yet, surprisingly, profit is rarely used as an objective: by only 7% of cases in the dataBANK and probably a lower percentage than this in the world at large. Setting explicit profit targets for marketing is difficult. For a start, there is the problem of defining the appropriate payback measures. There are as many incorrect measures of payback in use as there are (arguably) valid ones: this publication therefore includes a recommendation for a general definition and means of calculation (Part 7).

Then there is the problem of 'other factors'. Profits are affected by a host of factors besides marketing, on both the supply and the demand sides, making it hard to isolate the contribution of marketing.

To monitor the profit impact of marketing requires investment in the tools and techniques that can isolate its contribution, such as econometric modelling or regional testing. In general, therefore, profit is recommended as a *KPI* only where such a capability exists; but in these circumstances it is strongly recommended. Also, brands that do not have access to one of these tools are strongly recommended to invest in them, such are their benefits. This is especially true of econometric modelling. In general, the data argue for much more widespread use of econometric modelling as it clearly promotes both

The danger of setting ROI targets

Ambler (2004) wisely cautions against the setting of return on investment (ROI) targets (a commonly used profit metric). This can result in short-term budget cutting that will boost apparent ROI merely by reducing the level of investment. The net effect will be to harm longer-term profitability: an example of the potential danger of turning a metric into a target without adequate consideration. He advocates setting absolute profit targets – because achieving this will require optimised investment levels behind campaigns that generate good ROI results: 'If the I (investment) is constant then profit peaks at the same point that ROI does, so the ratio (i.e. ROI) is redundant at best and possibly misleading'. This is a good example of the importance of setting targets that avoid unwelcome tactics.

effectiveness and accountability of marketing, as well as (or perhaps because of) enabling a closer understanding of the drivers of profit growth. That is to say that **not only does the use of econometrics make the measurement of effect easier, but also, if used on an ongoing basis as part of the planning cycle, it makes subsequent campaigns more successful.** This point will be revisited in Part 6 (Measurement), but the top-line data largely speak for themselves (see Table 10).

Table 10: Power of econometric modelling	Full econometric model used	Other evaluation methods used
Incidence among all cases	15%	85%
Effectiveness success rate	81% (+++)	47%
Accountability success rate	74% (+)	58%

Nevertheless, even if there are no actual profit targets to be met, increasing profit should always be a primary objective for commercial campaigns. A clear strategy should be mapped out at the briefing stage for communications to achieve profit growth. This does not appear to be the case for most campaigns, and the result is marketing that underperforms (as shown in Table 8).

Fewer than 20% of marketers evaluate the profit effects of their communications*

Why is this? The answer almost certainly lies at the heart of the marketing accountability issue: a view has not been taken of what level of response constitutes an acceptable return on the investment made in the communications budget. Barwise (1999) suggests that, typically, half the return on communications investment for packaged goods brands is achieved in year one, with the remaining half coming through in years two to three. It should not be impossible in most situations to calculate an approximate required return (e.g. from sales or margin increases) to justify the budget. It helps no one to abstain from doing so and merely feeds the divide between finance or procurement and marketing. This divide was illustrated in a recent McKinsey study of CEOs (Marketing Society 2004), which reported a view of the marketing function as 'undisciplined', 'uncommercial' and 'not accountable'.

*Source: IPA 2005

Target market share, not sales

If profit should be the master objective, what should be the subsidiary ones? Table 8 revealed that sales gain is the single most common objective (62% of cases), and is nearly always a primary aim. Yet **campaigns that focus on sales significantly under-perform.** The table shows that they have the lowest overall success rate in terms of effectiveness and accountability. Table 11 reveals that they are less effective than average across every business metric.

In contrast, share gain as a KPI is generally much more likely to lead to a successful outcome than sales gain. **Campaigns that target market share are more effective – they significantly outperform sales-focused campaigns on every business metric.** (They are also more accountable, i.e. more likely to win prizes – see the Appendix.)

Table 11: Relative effectiveness of campaigns targeting share vs sales

% reporting very large effects on:	Average of all campaigns disclosing hard objectives	Campaigns aiming to increase sales	Campaigns aiming to increase share
Sales	45%	44%	58% (+++)
Market share	25%	24%	41% (+++)
Profit	23%	20%	26% (++)
Penetration	23%	19% (−)	33% (+++)
Loyalty	7%	5% (−)	10%
Price sensitivity	4%	2% (− −)	5%
Any measure	**55%**	**51% (− − −)**	**78% (+++)**

It is important, however, that market share is not pursued without the over-riding profit objective: Armstrong and Green (2007) have shown that if share alone is targeted then commonly, profitability is eroded (presumably because brand management teams are incentivised to buy share through promotions and pricing at the cost of profitability). So the PIMS findings should be modified with the proviso that ROI rises as market share grows only if share growth is obtained without discounting or other profit-diluting tactics.

The PIMS view of market share

It is worth noting that the recommendation to focus on market share (rather than sales) is corroborated by the highly authoritative PIMS database of over 3000 business units (Buzzell & Gale 1987). According to PIMS, market share is one of the most important drivers of company profitability: 'There is no doubt that market share and return on investment are strongly related. On average, market leaders can earn rates of return that are three times greater than businesses with a market share rank of fifth, or worse.'

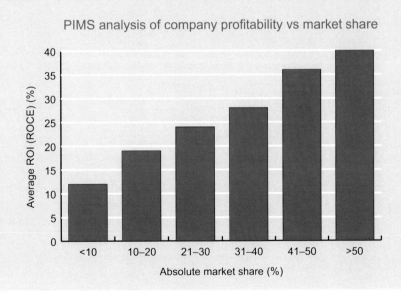

PIMS analysis of company profitability vs market share

Only in the case of small brands is increasing share a more dominant aim than increasing sales in practice. This is not surprising, but the data suggest that this should more widely be the case.

It is fairly obvious why IPA judges find market share gains more convincing than sales increases. It is not difficult to build brand sales in a growing market, for instance, but marketing may not be the cause. Trying to build market share is a much tougher task. **Market share is a much more accountable KPI than sales because it is not influenced by the state of the market.**

More subtly, the requirement to identify a source of share growth focuses the minds and strategy of the team, as well as ensuring that the strategy delivers in the way it was intended to. As a result, **campaigns that focus on market share tend to be more effective, as well as more accountable.**

Market share is therefore recommended as a KPI, rather than sales, for most brands. Exceptions would be:

- brands that have very high market shares (for which category, rather than share growth, may be a more sensible objective)
- brands that don't have well-defined competitive sets (for which market share may be misleading).

Focus on value, not volume

If market share should usually be the focal subsidiary objective to profit, the question arises of value share or volume?

The IPA dataBANK favours value share over volume because of the importance of relative pricing to profitability. Table 8 showed that trying to reduce price sensitivity is a very effective strategy. Campaigns that aim to reduce price sensitivity are much more likely to produce very large effects than those that focus on volume measures, and are more likely to win prizes. In particular, **reducing price sensitivity is, by a large margin, the most successful route to increasing profitability** (see Figure 6).

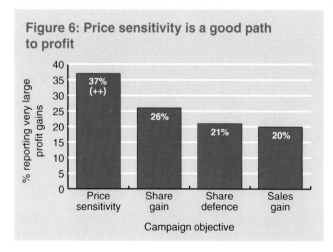

Figure 6: Price sensitivity is a good path to profit

Reducing price sensitivity seems to be a particularly profitable strategy for cheaper brands, presumably because small increases in price will have a larger effect on margins than for mainstream or premium brands.

Moreover, the fact that cases for which reducing price sensitivity was an objective enjoyed a very high success rate in the IPA Awards, suggests that this leads to greater accountability as well as profit. Lower price sensitivity also brings beneficial effects across a range of measures, including sales, loyalty and (reassuringly) price elasticity (see Table 12).

Table 12: The benefits of targeting price sensitivity and share

% reporting very large effects on:	Average of all campaigns disclosing hard objectives	Campaigns aiming to reduce price sensitivity	Campaigns aiming to increase share
Sales	45%	70% (+++)	58% (+++)
Market share	25%	33%	41% (+++)
Profit	23%	37% (++)	26% (++)
Penetration	23%	17%	33% (+++)
Loyalty	7%	17% (+++)	10%
Price sensitivity	4%	23% (+++)	5%
Any measure	**55%**	**83% (+++)**	**78% (+++)**

It's easy to see why price sensitivity is so important. Suppose you operate on a profit margin of 20%, and you have a choice between a) increasing volume by 1% while maintaining price, or b) maintaining volume while increasing price by 1%. Increasing price produces *five times* as much extra profit (see Table 13).

Table 13: Effect of 1% price increase vs 1% volume increase

	Base case	1% volume increase	1% price increase
Sales units	1,000,000	1,010,000	1,000,000
Price per unit	£1.00	£1.00	£1.01
Sales revenue	£1,000,000	£1,010,000	£1,010,000
Variable cost per unit	£0.80	£0.80	£0.80
Variable costs	£800,000	£808,000	£800,000
Marginal contribution	£200,000	£202,000	£210,000
Profit increase	–	**£2,000**	**£10,000**

Despite the all-round benefits of doing so, reducing price sensitivity is rarely an objective (only 4% of dataBANK cases). It is likely that the reasons for this are more to do with the difficulty of measuring price elasticity than lack of belief in its importance. Econometric modelling is needed to provide a reliable measure of price elasticity and places certain data requirements on the brand team; but surely the huge potential benefits of knowing optimum pricing for the brand must make the expenditure of

The PIMS view of pricing

Once again PIMS is enlightening: a further PIMS finding is that relative price (driven by perceived relative quality) is also an important driver of profitability. The implication of this is that value share, which includes the effect of relative pricing, should be a more effective KPI than volume share. It also favours strategies aimed at 'earning your way in' to greater market share (i.e. quality and service) rather than 'buying your way in' (i.e. heavy discounting). PIMS suggests that stronger relative pricing is a major benefit of successful marketing and a primary source of profit growth for brands in mature categories.

time and money worthwhile? There has certainly been a trend towards greater use of econometric modelling in the case studies of the dataBANK, and research among UK advertising agencies (IPA Best Practice Guide *'Evaluation'*, 2006) suggests that 55% now use econometric modelling on behalf of at least some of their clients. The clear evidence of this analysis (and others) is that reducing price elasticity should be a marketing objective for most brands in most categories. Therefore, unless loyalty and consumer pricing are not issues for the brand, **price elasticity (or alternatively relative price) is a recommended KPI.**

However, if it is not feasible to measure price elasticity, a sensible fallback is to use relative price as a KPI.

Given the importance of relative price to profitability, **value share is generally a more appropriate KPI than volume share, since it takes account of the impact of pricing to a degree.** Focusing on value makes it harder to 'buy' volume at the expense of profit.

The most common business KPIs are not the ideal ones

So, the overall conclusions of the dataBANK regarding business objectives are to target profit increase and/or reduced price sensitivity as primary objectives, generally to target share rather than sales as a subsidiary objective and to make value share the KPI rather than volume. In practice though, even among the examples in the dataBANK, this is not the case. The data demonstrate that sales gain is the most common objective – more than share gain and defence combined (62% vs 41%). Moreover the usual measures of share quoted are volume rather than value, implying a focus on the former. So the general pattern is in some ways the reverse of the ideal for effectiveness – even among the case studies of the dataBANK.

Behavioural objectives

Having set the primary objectives for the campaign in terms of business results, the behavioural changes needed to achieve those objectives must be identified. Behavioural objectives should generally be secondary. However, for some not-for-profit cases (e.g. government information campaigns), business measures are irrelevant, in which case behavioural measures should be primary.

Focus on penetration, not loyalty

Naturally, behavioural objectives vary widely, but nevertheless two very common goals are either to increase penetration or increase loyalty. Of these, the latter is more common.

However, the IPA dataBANK shows that **the loyalty approach only rarely leads to successful marketing outcomes. Loyalty campaigns underperform on almost every business metric, and win few prizes.** When they do work, the outcome is usually not greatly increased loyalty either (see Table 14). In fact, only 9% of loyalty campaigns actually increase loyalty significantly, not much higher than for non-loyalty campaigns. The explanation of this is discussed below and in Part 6 (Measurement).

By contrast, **penetration as an objective and route to share growth appears more frequently to lead to successful marketing outcomes.** Yet loyalty as an objective is actually *more than twice* as common as penetration.

Penetration campaigns do tend to increase penetration strongly (46% of cases), and they tend to do better than average on most of the other business metrics as well. This is consistent with a model of communications as a weak force in most scenarios (discussed in Part 6).

Table 14: The primacy of targeting penetration over loyalty

% reporting very large effects on:	Average of all campaigns disclosing hard objectives	Campaigns aiming to increase loyalty	Campaigns aiming to increase penetration
Sales	45%	35% (– –)	62% (+++)
Market share	25%	15% (– – –)	35% (+++)
Profit	23%	18%	31% (++)
Penetration	23%	15% (– –)	46% (+++)
Loyalty	7%	9%	7%
Price sensitivity	4%	4%	5%
Any measure	**55%**	**44% (– – –)**	**77% (+++)**

So, there is a strong conflict between the incidence of loyalty-building campaigns and their effectiveness vs penetration-building campaigns (see Figure 7).

Figure 7: Loyalty campaigns are more common than they should be

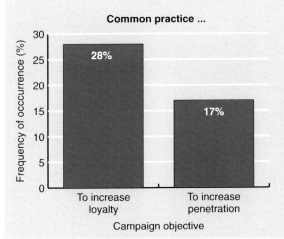

Although most campaigns focus on either penetration or loyalty, a few aim to increase both. The evidence from the dataBANK suggests that this can be quite effective, although penetration should still come first (see Table 15).

Table 15: Aiming for penetration and loyalty can be successful

	Campaign objective		
	Loyalty only	Loyalty and penetration	Penetration only
Incidence amongst all cases	22%	5%	12%
Effectiveness success rate	24% (– – –)	88% (+++)	73% (+++)
Accountability success rate	26% (– – –)	61% (++)	73% (+++)

However, despite this, campaigns that try to do both win no more prizes than those that focus only on penetration. Once again, it seems that setting more objectives makes accountability more challenging.

The dataBANK reveals why the solus pursuit of loyalty is relatively so fruitless. First, it is rare that loyalty growth alone is observed: where it is observed it usually accompanies penetration growth, but it is much more likely that penetration growth alone will be observed (see Figure 8).

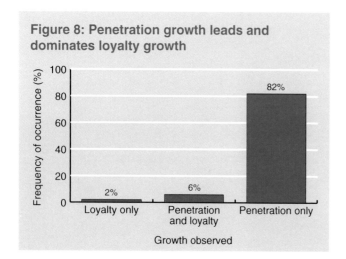

Figure 8: Penetration growth leads and dominates loyalty growth

Second, where growth of both loyalty and penetration are recorded, penetration is usually the greater effect (see Figure 9).

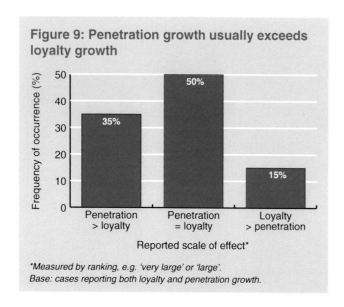

Figure 9: Penetration growth usually exceeds loyalty growth

*Measured by ranking, e.g. 'very large' or 'large'.
Base: cases reporting both loyalty and penetration growth.

So, the overall conclusion here is that, in general, **penetration is a more fertile objective than loyalty and a recommended KPI where share growth is also an objective.** Moreover, especially for brands operating in repertoire categories, loyalty is a much less sensible objective, and much less useful as a KPI.

The Ehrenberg view on loyalty

Andrew Ehrenberg has studied the workings of numerous categories for almost 50 years and developed mathematical models (Dirichlet models) that explain observed adoption and usage patterns of brands by consumers. The dataBANK findings on buying behaviour echo those of Ehrenberg (2000). His analysis, based on his many years of research, suggests that penetration has a much bigger impact than loyalty on market share, and that attempts to increase loyalty without increasing penetration are largely futile. He therefore recommends that marketers concentrate on penetration rather than loyalty. A common criticism of the Ehrenberg team's work is that it is focused on fmcg markets. Categories such as durables are different, it is argued, and loyalty plays a more important role. This criticism is not entirely fair – Ehrenberg has found similar results in some durables and services markets (Ehrenberg 2005), but his evidence is too limited for some.

As might be expected, the dataBANK shows that **increasing penetration is a particularly effective strategy for newly launched brands, small brands, and brands in new and fast-growing categories**. In these contexts there is the most scope to increase penetration.

While trying to increase loyalty is generally harder, the dataBANK suggests that it may be worth trying for big brands, presumably because the scope for increasing penetration is limited. Increasing loyalty is also more likely to succeed for cheaper brands: this may be because of the capacity to reduce price sensitivity and hence increase apparent loyalty, as discussed before. And increasing loyalty seems to be easier in categories where the purchase decision is more emotional than rational.

Supporting evidence for the Ehrenberg doctrine from outside of fmcg appears to have been thin on the ground up until now. The dataBANK is able to shed new light on the issue, and it appears that the finding is fairly universal. **Trying to increase penetration appears to be more successful than trying to increase loyalty, regardless of category** (see Table 16).

Table 16

Effectiveness success rates (% reporting very large business effects) of campaigns aiming:	Category			
	fmcg	Durables	Services	Not-for-profit
To increase loyalty	55% (–)	43% (–)	29% (– –)	13%
To increase penetration	77% (+++)	82%	87% (+++)	33% (+)

This holds true even in the most testing situation of 'subscription services' – service markets where customers effectively lock themselves into a brand for the duration of their relationship (e.g. fixed and mobile communications, financial services, ISPs, and so on). Customers in these categories do not generally operate a purchase repertoire: any brand promiscuity must, of necessity, be serial in nature, not parallel. Moreover, brand comparison in these categories is complex and suppresses any tendency to switch. Nevertheless the evidence of the dataBANK suggests that even these brands are better off focusing their communications on penetration rather than loyalty building or reducing churn. If anything, the data suggest that penetration gains are even more likely to yield strong business results than for service brands in general. **This does not mean that loyalty is irrelevant, or that firms should ignore their existing customers in favour of new ones**. Some marketing that attempts to build loyalty does turn out to be highly profitable. But the dataBANK suggests that when such 'loyalty campaigns' *do* work, they do so mainly by recruiting new customers, not by reducing churn or by extracting more

A world that revolves around you

Loyalty rewarded. O₂

The 2006 O₂ mobile telecommunications case study reports the effects of a new campaign aiming to reduce churn and increase usage by announcing rewards for loyalty. Was this an exception to the Ehrenberg loyalty doctrine? The case study reports an impressive reduction in churn, but it also reports an equally impressive growth in penetration; if you do the maths, it appears that around two-thirds of share growth came from new customers and one-third from reduced churn. The strengthening of intermediate measures relating to penetration growth was also more impressive than of those relating to loyalty. There is no doubting the considerable effectiveness of the O₂ campaign, but it doesn't disprove the Ehrenberg doctrine.

value from existing ones. Clearly making customers feel more highly valued will make them more likely to recommend the brand to others. But also, demonstrating publicly to non-customers that a company values and rewards its existing customers can itself be a powerful recruiter of new customers: this is likely to be a more commercially valuable effect than any loyalty growth. Both the O₂ and Tesco case studies demonstrate this. But the evidence from the dataBANK is that pursuing loyalty as a marketing objective in itself (in isolation of attracting new customers) is unlikely to be profitable.

Interestingly, the few very large loyalty gains achieved in packaged goods markets tended to be in categories/segments defined or dominated by a single idiosyncratic brand at the time (e.g. Marmite, Häagen-Dazs, Cadbury's Creme Eggs, Jammie Dodgers, Solvite). The definition of loyalty is a moot point in such situations: share of which category requirements? This suggests caution should be adopted in measuring loyalty in such categories, but again doesn't undermine the fundamental validity of the Ehrenberg doctrine.

Loyalty and customer relationship management (CRM)

The findings here run counter to a strong current in modern marketing practice. For decades it has been a truism among many in the marketing world that, because a brand's most loyal customers are its most valuable customers, marketing should focus on them. Indeed, the whole CRM movement is to some extent based on this assumption. The work of Bain & Co and of McKinsey & Co has been strongly influential here – in particular the often quoted findings of the former that a 5% improvement in customer retention can cause an increase in profitability of between 25% and 85%. This, of course, may well be true as a thought experiment, just as the conversion of lead into gold would be highly profitable, but, as the data show, it may be similarly elusive.

The dataBANK shows how pervasive this thinking has become: loyalty campaigns are almost twice as common as penetration campaigns. Yet the dataBANK, like Ehrenberg's work, suggests that this is far from ideal for effectiveness. And McKinsey has reported that the results of loyalty programmes for retailers are often disappointing (McKinsey & Co 2000), despite the fact that retailers have arguably the greatest scope for loyalty building of any brands. In fact, Ehrenberg's work suggests that, when marketing works, the payback mostly comes from the 'long tail' of non-users and light users. His work deserves greater attention among the marketing community and is revisited in Part 6 (Measurement).

A better measure of loyalty

In Table 12 (page 27), it was shown that campaigns aiming to reduce price sensitivity performed strongly at building loyalty. In fact, comparison with Table 14 shows that price sensitivity campaigns out-perform (by a significant margin of 17% vs 9%) those aiming to increase loyalty, in terms of very large loyalty effects. Both types of campaign perform similarly at penetration growth, so this is unlikely to be a factor. It is perhaps because the type of case study authors are reporting here is not loyalty defined in the traditional sense (share of category requirements), but rather the resilience of the brand's market share to competitive activity. It is a consequence of lower price sensitivity that a brand would suffer less during a period of heavy promotional activity by its competitors. In turn, this would manifest itself as an apparent increase in share of category purchasing over time. Given the observation that share of category requirements as a measure of loyalty is not influenced strongly by communications campaigns, whereas price sensitivity can be, the logical conclusion is that **'price sensitivity' is a better measure of marketing-induced loyalty than traditional 'share of category requirements'**.

Intermediate objectives

It was observed earlier (see Figure 4, page 20) that campaign objectives should generally be specified in terms of 'hard' results, rather than intermediate ones (beliefs, attitudes and awareness). This is just as true for not-for-profit brands as it is for commercial ones. The aim of marketing is almost always to change people's behaviour, not just what they think and feel. Campaigns that fail to specify hard objectives tend to be less effective (presumably because they are less focused) and less accountable (because it is harder to judge success or failure). This should be borne in mind when considering intermediate metrics.

Intermediate objectives are secondary

The main purpose of intermediate objectives should be as stepping-stones to the intended behavioural effects. So, if intermediate objectives are set, they should nearly always be secondary to the hard objectives. Table 17 demonstrates how much more effective and accountable campaigns are that do this, rather than making intermediate objectives primary.

Table 17: Hierarchy of campaign objectives	Intermediate objectives primary	Intermediate objectives secondary
Effectiveness success rate	37% (– – –)	74% (++)
Accountability success rate	39% (– – –)	60%

Any intermediate targets set should reflect the model of communications effect that has been adopted. For example, if brand awareness has been identified as a limiting factor for trial, then the objectives might be 'to increase market share by encouraging trial through increased brand awareness'. Brand awareness is always a means to an end, not an end in itself. **The value of intermediate measures is largely diagnostic or as leading indicators of expected business success. Ultimately, success or failure should be judged using hard measures.**

However, the dataBANK evidences the widespread use of intermediate targets as primary KPIs (24% of cases). The attractiveness of intermediate KPIs perhaps lies in their relative ease of measurement, as well as the fact that attitude or awareness shifts can be closely related to marketing activity. The best-known example of this is the Millward Brown Awareness Index, which measures the ability of the campaign to generate awareness of itself. This is unlikely to be a bad measure per se, but unfortunately suffers from the same problems as all intermediate measures: they do not directly relate to actual sales or profit generated. Moreover, the evidence of the dataBANK (and independently of ACNielsen, see Figure 31 in Part 6, Measurement) is that such measures do not always correlate with effectiveness and are unreliable in predicting hard results. The supporting evidence for this conclusion is presented and discussed in more detail in Part 6. Consequently perhaps, the use of intermediate measures does not correlate with accountability: that is to say, with prize winning in the IPA Awards.

There is also a growing school of thought that such high-cognition metrics do not measure the capacity of campaigns to generate low-attention processing (LAP). The theory advanced by adherents of LAP (principally Robert Heath) suggests that the majority of the long-term effects of campaigns may be due to their LAP strength. Conventional intermediate measures are therefore likely to misread the long-term potential of a campaign. The issue of LAP is revisited in more detail in Part 6.

Changing consumer attitudes only truly constitutes a valid primary objective in some not-for-profit cases such as government information campaigns, where sales and other commercial hard measures do not exist and behaviour is difficult to measure. In these situations, attitude shifts are a proxy for the intended behaviours that are desired, but if behavioural measures are available they should take precedence as KPIs. Attitude-related KPIs should, therefore, measure the ultimate attitude shift required (e.g. reduced interest in trying drugs), rather than 'softer' intermediate objectives (e.g. belief that drugs are harmful). The 1998 Health Education Authority Drugs Education Campaign case study is a good illustration of this, building its case largely on behavioural metrics backed up by only the hardest of attitudinal measures. The reason this is better is that it offers the best route to improve the otherwise poor correlation between intermediate measures and hard effects.

In general therefore, caution is advised over the use of intermediate metrics except as leading indicators or in the case of not-for-profit brands. The issue of how to make best use of intermediate metrics is revisited in Part 6.

Intermediate communications objectives are not equally productive

In terms of intermediate (communications) objectives, the data classify campaign objectives in the ways shown in Table 18; though campaigns can have more than one objective and they are rated as primary or secondary.

These classifications should not be confused with the communications models discussed in Part 4 (Communications strategy): they are objectives not *modus operandi* (although clearly one would expect to find linkage between the primary communications objectives of a campaign and the strategic model used).

The data in Table 19 illustrate the danger of evaluating campaigns purely against their intermediate objectives. Two communications goals are strikingly more likely to lead to success against the intended objective than others: campaigns targeting awareness and those directly influencing behaviour ('direct') have a good track record of demonstrating success against their goals (see Table 19). However, these goals tend to lead to fewer other beneficial intermediate effects, especially compared to fame-building campaigns.

Table 18: Communications objectives

Objective	Definition
Awareness	Building brand awareness/knowledge
Image	Creating brand values or user imagery that strengthen the brand's relationship with consumers
Direct*	Directly influencing behaviour such as trial or direct response, or overcoming barriers to purchase
Differentiation	Differentiation or vitality, setting the brand apart
Fame	Building the 'fame' of the brand or perceptions of its strength or authority – that is, the brand defines the category
Quality	Building a belief in the esteem and perceived quality of the brand
Commitment	Building commitment to the brand, a feeling of loyalty, brand relevance
Trust	Building a sense of trust or security in the brand

*'Direct' includes, but is not limited to, direct-response campaigns with a specific response step such as a phone number or transactional website. Direct influence includes promotional offers and other short-term sales messages.

Table 19: Success rates of achieving intermediate objectives and their breadth of effect

	Incidence among all cases	Success rate vs objective*	Average number of very large intermediate effects
Awareness	**61%**	**45% (+ + +)**	**1.8**
Image	55%	27% (– –)	1.7
Direct	**46%**	**46% (+ + +)**	**1.8**
Differentiation	43%	35%	2.0
Fame	33%	37%	2.3
Quality	33%	28% (–)	2.0
Commitment	31%	26% (– –)	1.9
Trust	22%	12% (– – –)	2.2

* Percentage of cases pursuing stated objective that reported very large effects on that measure.

Moreover, looking at business results (see Table 20) reveals that **the effectiveness success rates (i.e. the business effectiveness) of 'awareness' and 'direct' campaigns are among the lowest.** They are easy to evaluate against their intermediate objectives (and hence more accountable) but, if anything, less effective in business terms: the benefits of these objectives are therefore illusory.

Generally, differences in the business effectiveness of the various communications objectives are much less marked than differences in intermediate effects. They appear to make little difference to success, which is much more strongly determined by the hard objectives of the campaign. The significance of this is discussed in Part 4 (Communications strategy), but it suggests that **campaigns can work in a number of different ways, whatever the circumstances.**

Table 20: Success rates of intermediate objectives

	Incidence among all cases	Effectiveness success rate (% reporting very large business effects)	Accountability success rate (% winning awards)
Awareness	61%	67%	68%
Image	55%	68%	66%
Direct	46%	67%	71%
Differentiation	43%	70%	67%
Fame	33%	78% (++)	65%
Quality	33%	73%	65%
Commitment	31%	70%	61% (−)
Trust	22%	72%	60% (−)

So, it is not the case that targeting awareness necessarily leads to more commercially effective marketing (it does not, as is demonstrated in the table), merely that awareness is a more achievable objective. By an understandable coincidence, it is also the most common objective: a classic illustration of the potential downside of undisciplined target setting. The same is true to a lesser degree of 'direct' campaigns. Clearly, clients and agencies focus on these objectives not because they promote business success (if anything, they produce slightly smaller business effects), but because they are more accountable: it is easier to demonstrate corresponding intermediate effects, as a result of which they win more prizes. This reveals a tension between accountability and effectiveness. **What is easy to measure is not necessarily the best thing to do**.

More intermediate objectives are also good for effectiveness but not accountability

The number of intermediate objectives set also illustrates this tension. Some campaigns specify multiple communications objectives – for example, to build brand awareness and to improve quality perceptions. **Campaigns with multiple intermediate objectives tend to be more effective, but less accountable** (see Table 21).

Table 21: Success rates of numbers of soft objectives

	1	2–3	4+
Effectiveness success rate	54% (− −)	61%	75% (++)
Accountability success rate	81% (++)	77% (+)	58% (− − −)

The power of fame

The one notable exception in Table 20 to this picture of relatively uniform effectiveness of objectives is 'fame' – the authority of the brand in its category. Building brand fame as an objective (and as a communications strategy, as will be demonstrated in Part 4) leads to significantly more effective campaigns with broader multiple effects. **Campaigns targeting brand fame outperform others on all business metrics, particularly market share growth** (see Table 22). It is perhaps not surprising that this is particularly the case with brand launches and for smaller brands in general.

Table 22: Effects of campaign objectives

% reporting very large effects on:	Average of all campaigns disclosing intermediate objectives	Campaigns aiming to build brand fame	Campaigns aiming to build brand awareness
Sales	49%	55% (+)	51%
Market share	33%	40% (++)	34%
Profit	24%	28%	22%
Penetration	31%	35%	31%
Loyalty	11%	16% (+)	8% (−)
Price sensitivity	5%	6%	4%
Any measure	**69%**	**78% (++)**	**67%**

The data would argue for more widespread adoption of fame as an objective, yet it is squeezed into a poor fifth position in the league table of incidence, behind less effective objectives such as brand awareness and brand image.

Fame is not the same as awareness – it is a perception of authority in the category rather than a state of knowledge – so it is not surprising that awareness, as an objective, does not yield the same level of efficacy in campaigns. In fact awareness as an objective yields weaker results across the entire range of effects. One hypothesis (in part supported by the pattern of effects) is that the potency of fame lies partly in its ability to raise the relative perceived quality of the brand – not necessarily in a rational (product performance) sense, but rather in an emotional (belief in the brand) sense.

Campaigns targeting fame are significantly more effective than those targeting awareness, yet the latter are more accountable (win more prizes). It is likely that this is because awareness is easier to measure and probably explains why brand awareness is by far the most popular communications objective, accounting for 61% of all cases.

Targeting quality is more important than image

If brand awareness is the most common communications goal, brand image comes a close second; 52% of campaigns aim to 'create brand values or user imagery that strengthen the brand's relationship with consumers'. **Yet, despite their popularity, brand image campaigns are not particularly effective. Nor are they very accountable.** Anyone who has ever followed a tracking study over a period of years will attest that important brand image measures don't usually move very much, even when the campaign seems to be working. In fact, only 27% of image campaigns actually report very large shifts in brand image, making image shift one of the hardest objectives to achieve (see Table 19).

Perhaps it pays to be more specific. Campaigns that aim to differentiate the brand from the competition, or that aim to build quality perceptions, generally do slightly better than those that merely try to build a strong brand image (see Table 23).

In particular, trying to improve quality perceptions seems to be a good idea if you want to reduce price sensitivity. It has already been shown that supporting a price premium can be highly profitable, so it's not surprising to find that **quality-enhancing campaigns are, along with fame-building campaigns, the**

Table 23: Quality is more potent than image

% reporting very large effects on:	Average of all campaigns disclosing intermediate objectives	Campaigns aiming to build brand image	Campaigns aiming to improve perceptions of brand quality
Sales	49%	48%	47%
Market share	33%	31%	32%
Profit	24%	25%	28%
Penetration	31%	28%	30%
Loyalty	11%	10%	14%
Price sensitivity	5%	5%	7%
Any measure	**69%**	**68%**	**73%**

most profitable. This accords with the PIMS research, which showed that quality perceptions are a key driver of profitability, because of their effect on the ability to maintain stronger pricing.

Of course, for some of the most effective campaigns, brand fame and quality perceptions go hand in hand (see below).

The Marks & Spencer fame campaign

The 2006 Marks & Spencer fame campaign built quality and innovation perceptions and led to a 7% increase in footfall and overall sales.

Commitment and trust are weak objectives

If fame merits note as a relatively effective objective, then building commitment and trust merit note as relatively weak objectives. This is not to say that they cannot lead to effective campaigns, but they are significantly less likely to lead to positive business outcomes in general. Given that commitment and trust tend to go hand in hand with loyalty as a business objective, it is not surprising that they under-perform in business terms. Indeed, the one area where they perform relatively strongly is in improving brand loyalty, but even on that narrow measure they do not outperform fame campaigns, and in common with all campaigns they rarely achieve it (see Table 24).

There is some evidence that trust is slightly more important for brand launches and brands in newer categories. This is consistent with consumers being on less familiar ground in these situations. Brand trust is also slightly more important for budget brands, presumably because consumers may be wary that low cost implies unreliability.

Table 24: Commitment and trust perform weakly

% reporting very large effects on:	Average of all campaigns disclosing intermediate objectives	Campaigns aiming to build brand commitment	Campaigns aiming to build brand trust	Campaigns aiming to build brand fame
Sales	49%	40% (– –)	46%	55% (+)
Market share	33%	30%	36%	40% (++)
Profit	24%	24%	21%	28%
Penetration	31%	29%	31%	35%
Loyalty	11%	16% (+)	17% (+)	16% (+)
Price sensitivity	5%	5%	4%	6%
Any measure	**69%**	**70%**	**72%**	**78% (++)**

Direct campaigns have limited effects, but are profitable

It has already been demonstrated that campaigns that aim to directly influence consumers (e.g. direct response campaigns and promotional campaigns) are more accountable (Table 20). It is likely that this is linked to their good track record of producing the direct effects they seek (Table 19). Yet direct campaigns are the least likely to produce very large business effects. On most metrics, they are poor to average, and compare poorly with fame campaigns (see Table 25).

Table 25: Direct campaigns yield fewer very large business effects

% reporting very large effects on:	Average of all campaigns disclosing intermediate objectives	Campaigns aiming to directly influence behaviour	Campaigns aiming to build brand fame
Sales	49%	49%	55% (+)
Market share	33%	30%	40% (++)
Profit	24%	27%	28%
Penetration	31%	32%	35%
Loyalty	11%	8%	16% (+)
Price sensitivity	5%	5%	6%
Any measure	**69%**	**67%**	**78% (++)**

However, direct campaigns perform above average on profit generation (up there with fame-building campaigns). This is not necessarily a contradiction. Direct campaigns may not produce such large effects, but what effects they do yield tend to be generated in a cost-effective and more immediate way. In other words, **direct campaigns may not be as broadly effective as others, but they may be more efficient (in terms of short-term profit generation)**. Clearly, a number of very successful businesses have been built using direct campaigns (e.g. Direct Line and Dell computers), but they have also tended to benefit from different business models that create strong consumer price offers capable of offsetting any communications weaknesses.

Summary: golden rules for briefing

1. Set clear campaign objectives, ideally quantified, with timescales.

2. For maximum effectiveness, spell out objectives in detail, but recognise that for maximum accountability the number of objectives is best minimised.

3. Focus on the objectives that matter. KPIs should be based on hard objectives and prioritised. Business KPIs should come first, behavioural KPIs second.

4. For commercial campaigns, profit should usually be the ultimate goal. Make this explicit, even if it is not practical to set actual profit targets.

5. Use market share as your KPI, rather than sales, unless your market is difficult to define, your market share is unusually high, or you are trying to grow the market.

6. Set KPIs in terms of value, rather than volume.

7. Focus on penetration as a KPI, rather than a 'loyalty' measure (such as share of category requirement), unless penetration is already maximised.

8. Price sensitivity is a better measure of loyalty. Reducing price sensitivity can be highly profitable, especially for cheaper brands and brands with high penetration. If price elasticity is not a practical KPI, monitor relative price and value share.

9. Intermediate attitudinal or awareness objectives are usually only the means to an end; intermediate KPIs are best used for diagnosis and as leading indicators.

10. Campaigns can work in many different ways. Tailor your KPIs to the way your campaign works.

11. Brand awareness can be a useful metric, but aiming for brand fame is more effective.

12. Aim to improve quality perceptions rather than merely improve brand image, particularly if you are trying to reduce price sensitivity.

13. Brand trust is a poor KPI, except when dealing with small brands, budget brands and new categories.

14. Direct response metrics help make a campaign accountable. However, direct campaigns, while cost-effective in profit terms, tend to produce fewer business effects.

3 Budget setting

This section will recommend a task-based approach for setting budgets (i.e. a 'zero-based' approach in which budgets are determined by the brand's business objectives and anticipated competitive activity). It will set out a fairly straightforward method for budget setting that does not require complex analysis or econometric modelling, though the benefits of econometric modelling in budget setting are evident. Other ways in which budgets can be set will be reviewed and their deficiencies relative to the recommended approach observed.

Share of voice should reflect market share targets

Clearly, budgets cannot sensibly be set in isolation of objectives (and vice versa). The bolder the objectives, in general, the larger the budget required. As discussed in Part 2, **share of market (SOM) is usually one of the best KPIs to use when it comes to setting objectives**.

Budgets should also reflect the competitive context. The more your competitors are spending, the more you will need to spend to compete with them. For this reason, **share of voice (SOV) is usually a better KPI than absolute spend when it comes to setting budgets.** The dataBANK shows that SOV is strongly correlated with brand performance, whereas absolute size of budget is not (see Appendix).

It is a well-established fact of marketing life that expenditure (in the shape of SOV) needs to reflect desired SOM. Several authors have proposed that there are general relationships between market share and SOV (e.g. Broadbent 1989; Jones 1990; Buck 2001), and that for any given market share there is an equilibrium SOV at which that market share will be stable. If SOV is above the equilibrium level, then market share will generally rise to the new higher equilibrium level. Similarly, if SOV falls below the equilibrium level, then market share will generally fall. This is illustrated conceptually in Figure 10.

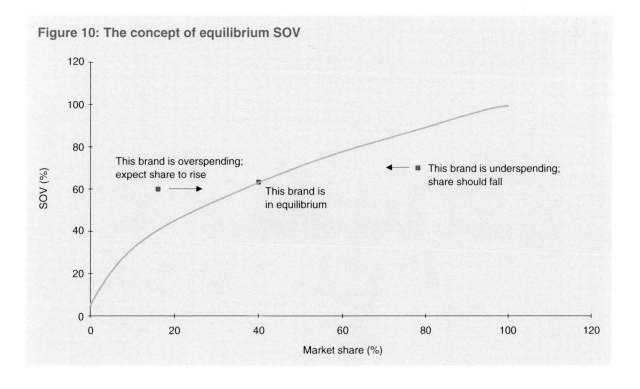

Figure 10: The concept of equilibrium SOV

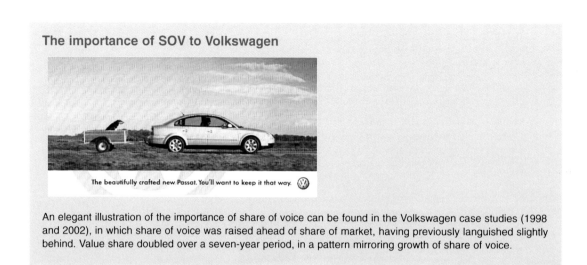

The importance of SOV to Volkswagen

The beautifully crafted new Passat. You'll want to keep it that way.

An elegant illustration of the importance of share of voice can be found in the Volkswagen case studies (1998 and 2002), in which share of voice was raised ahead of share of market, having previously languished slightly behind. Value share doubled over a seven-year period, in a pattern mirroring growth of share of voice.

Various studies have corroborated this 'law' by demonstrating a correlation between market share and share of voice, most notably:

- Jones (1990) examining 1096 brands in 23 countries, and
- Buck (2001) examining UK brand leaders in 26 fmcg categories over the period 1975–1999.

Buck's data are presented graphically in Figure 11.

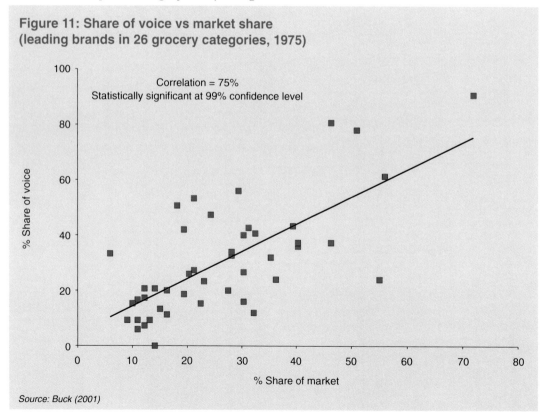

Figure 11: Share of voice vs market share (leading brands in 26 grocery categories, 1975)

Correlation = 75%
Statistically significant at 99% confidence level

Source: Buck (2001)

The IPA dataBANK also corroborates this general relationship (for varied brands of many categories and sizes, not just fmcg category leaders), revealing a good correlation between a brand's

SOV during a campaign and the final market share resulting (see Figure 12). This is despite the much greater diversity of the brands and categories included in the dataBANK than of Buck's more homogeneous sample.

In Part 2 of this publication, it was argued that **market share by value is a better KPI than market share by volume**, since it takes some account of the effects of marketing on price. On this basis, one would expect share of voice to correlate more strongly with value share than volume, and this is indeed the case. Figure 12 is primarily based on value data, although volume figures have been used for those cases where value is not available.

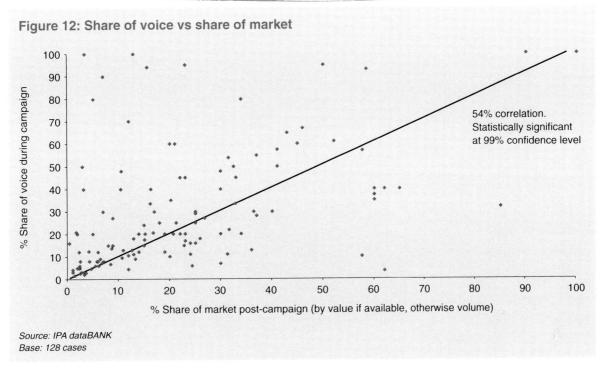

Figure 12: Share of voice vs share of market

54% correlation. Statistically significant at 99% confidence level

% Share of voice during campaign

% Share of market post-campaign (by value if available, otherwise volume)

Source: IPA dataBANK
Base: 128 cases

As a rough rule of thumb for budget setting, the data suggest that, **for successful brands, share of voice tends to be roughly equal to value share of market**. However, it is immediately obvious from Figure 12 that there is a fair amount of variation either side of the best-fit line – that there are many brands that have chosen to spend above or below the 'equilibrium level', yet have still achieved some level of commercial success (as evidenced by their presence in the dataBANK). So it is important to understand more precisely the nature of the relationship between share of voice and share of market.

Eagle-eyed readers may have noticed the somewhat fan-shaped distribution of outliers around the line. Brands sitting above the line have SOV greater than SOM, whereas brands below the line have SOV less than SOM. Theory suggests that brands sitting above the line should outperform those sitting below it. The dataBANK confirms that this is indeed the case.

The best way to illustrate this is to calculate the 'excess' share of voice – the difference between SOV and SOM. Figure 13 shows a good correlation between share growth (vertical axis) and this excess SOV (horizontal axis). The bigger the excess share of voice, the faster a brand tends to grow.

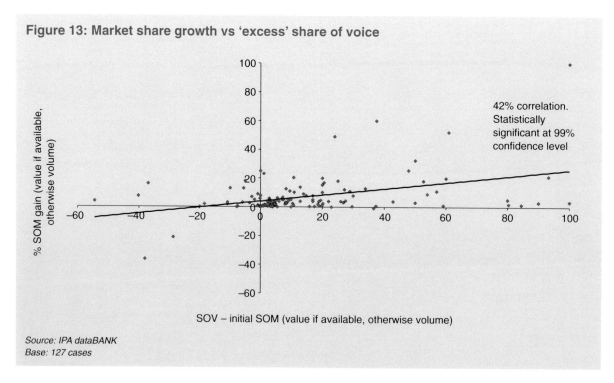

Figure 13: Market share growth vs 'excess' share of voice

y-axis: % SOM gain (value if available, otherwise volume)

x-axis: SOV – initial SOM (value if available, otherwise volume)

42% correlation. Statistically significant at 99% confidence level

Source: IPA dataBANK
Base: 127 cases

In other words, **the higher SOV is above SOM, the faster market share grows** – and of course the reverse. This makes intuitive sense, and it turns out that the best predictor of growth is the excess SOV at the *beginning* of the campaign, not the end. This finding is important for two reasons.

First, it shows that the relationship is truly causal. Share growth tends to follow high levels of share of voice, not vice versa. Other authors have found similar time lags, proving that SOV really does drive market share, not the other way around. Indeed, Buck (2001) found evidence of quite long-term effects of SOV on growth.

Second, it indicates that the **initial excess SOV is an important KPI when it comes to setting budgets, since this is what determines the rate of growth**.

Figure 13 suggests that share growth is in fact roughly proportional to excess SOV. Averaging across all the cases in the IPA dataBANK, every 10 points of excess SOV seem to generate around 2.2 percentage points of extra share growth.

However, it should be borne in mind that IPA campaigns are, by their very nature, more effective than average. One would expect a 'typical' campaign to generate somewhat less growth for any given level of share of voice. Fortunately, a technique called Tobit analysis allows extrapolation from the IPA data to estimate the relationship between growth and SOV for the wider population, by recognising that our sample has been restricted to cases showing growth (see Appendix for details). Tobit analysis suggests that, for an 'average' campaign, 10 points of excess SOV generate around one point of extra share growth. In other words, it seems that **IPA cases are probably more than twice as effective as the average campaign**.

The data therefore suggest the following rule of thumb: that **for every point of market share a brand seeks to gain, its share of voice needs to be around 10 points above its market share**. A number of

Marketing in the Era of Accountability

other studies have shown very similar relationships between share growth and SOV–SOM; these are summarised in Table 26, and some are charted in the accompanying box on page 46.

Table 26: Estimated share growth resulting from 10-point surplus SOV over SOM

Data source	Category	Share growth (% points)
Peckham	Unknown	1.3
DDB	Margarine	1.2
DDB	Durables category A	1.0
Millward Brown	Various	1.0
IPA dataBANK	Various	1.0
DDB	Mobile phones	0.9
DDB	Cosmetics	0.5
DDB	Durables category B	0.2
Average	**See above**	**0.9**

Further corroboration comes from reported advertising 'elasticities' (though for technical reasons it is arguably not helpful to describe the relationship between advertising and sales as an 'elasticity' and so it is avoided in this publication). The advertising 'elasticity' is defined as the percentage change in sales that results from a 1% change in the advertising budget. The dataBANK analysis suggests that the advertising 'elasticity' is probably around 0.1 for an 'average' campaign. And indeed, other researchers regularly report that typical 'elasticities' are around 0.1 (e.g. Tellis (2007) reported a range from 0.05 to 0.1).

So the dataBANK general rule of thumb for share of voice is well corroborated by other research.

There are some interesting apparent implications of this general relationship that are worth examining.

First, that it is *share of voice*, rather than budget size, that most accurately predicts success, and therefore some view of likely competitive expenditure must be factored in to budgeting.

Second, that **for most brands, most of the marketing budget serves to maintain market share, rather than to create growth**. The proportion of the marketing budget that does create growth rises with the level of the budget above the equilibrium level. To illustrate this, imagine that a brand's equilibrium SOV is 10% and that its actual SOV is 15%. In this case two-thirds (10 ÷ 15) of the budget is spent maintaining equilibrium and one-third achieving growth. Next imagine that SOV is increased by a third to 20% – now *half* the budget is creating growth. The misleading consequence of this is that if return on marketing investment is simplistically viewed as (value of growth) ÷ (cost of marketing) then return on marketing investment will apparently rise with spend. **It is therefore important to note that (value of growth) ÷ (cost of marketing) is in fact an invalid definition of return** that fails to acknowledge that the effects of marketing are first to maintain market share (or to slow decline) and only then (SOV permitting) to produce growth. For this reason Part 7 describes how to reliably

Other studies examining growth vs SOV–SOM

Table 26 shows that the dataBANK result is very close to the cross-category average, as one would hope. In particular, the Millward Brown study (Twose 2005), the only other multi-category study available (based on over 300 cases), found a similar relationship between SOV and growth.

Millward Brown analysis of share growth vs SOV–SOM

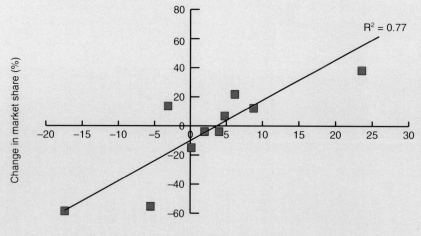

Relative share of voice (%)

Source: Millward Brown

Twose reports that the correlation can be improved by adjusting SOV for the standout power of the campaign (its Awareness Index) – he refers to this as 'effective SOV'.

The Peckham (1974) study (of an unknown brand) for Unilever also showed a very similar correlation to the dataBANK.

Share growth vs (SOV – share)

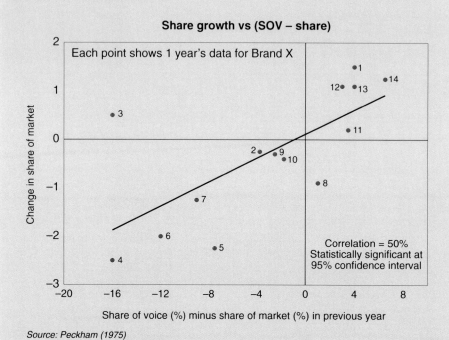

Share of voice (%) minus share of market (%) in previous year

Source: Peckham (1975)

calculate profit return so that it includes the negative consequences of no expenditure (the true baseline for value of growth).

Third, that absolute spend in excess of the maintenance level buys an absolute amount of share growth. This would be broadly consistent with growth in the weak theory (explained in Part 6), because it argues that advertising's main role in growth is the recruitment of new users and thus growth comes from greater saliency among category users as a whole; this in turn would be a factor of *absolute* increases in SOV, not *relative* increases. This would imply that the benefit of excess share of voice in terms of share points of growth would not vary with the size of the brand.

However, although growth is not proportional to the size of the brand, closer inspection of the data reveal that larger brands do enjoy an advantage over smaller ones.

Required budget also depends on the size of the brand

So far a linear relationship between stable market share and share of voice has been suggested; however, on closer inspection it appears that the relationship is not entirely linear. A better fit can be obtained if, as market share increases, the required equilibrium share of voice flattens off (see Figure 14).

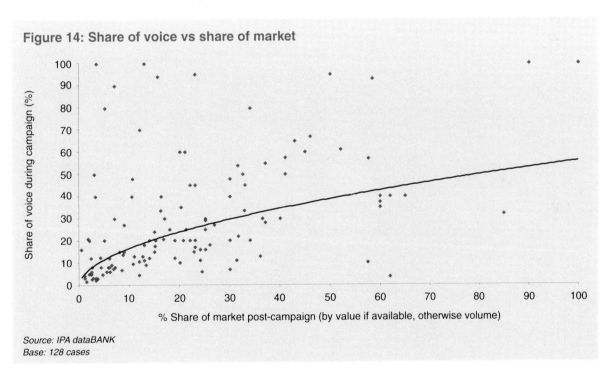

Figure 14: Share of voice vs share of market

Source: IPA dataBANK
Base: 128 cases

Very similar results have been found in some of DDB's unpublished studies (see Figure 15).

This non-linearity implies that **big brands can get away with spending a smaller proportion of their revenues on communications.** A corollary of this is that advertising-to-spend ratios are a somewhat flawed metric for budget setting, because they assume that all brands in a category should work to the same ratio.

Jones (1990) found a similar result in his study of 1096 fmcg brands. Figure 16 shows that small brands tend to set SOV above SOM, while big brands tend to set it below.

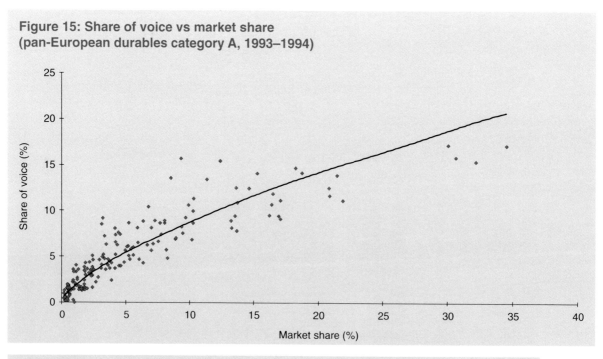

Figure 15: Share of voice vs market share (pan-European durables category A, 1993–1994)

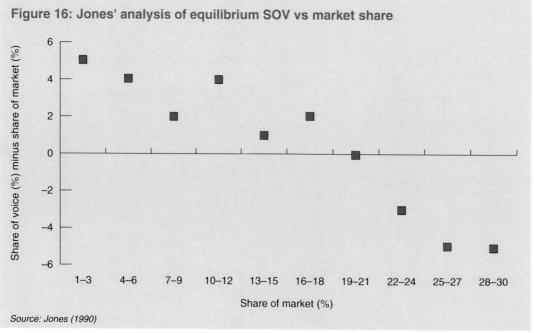

Figure 16: Jones' analysis of equilibrium SOV vs market share

Source: Jones (1990)

In part, this probably reflects various economies of scale. Big brands tend to have advantages in terms of price, distribution and innovation, which may mean they don't have to rely quite so strongly on advertising to maintain market share. Jones' data suggested that brands with market share in excess of 25% could get away with a share of voice around 5% lower than market share, whereas brands with less than 10% market share typically needed a share of voice around 4% above market share to 'hold their own'. This in turn means that advertising by existing category players can act as a significant barrier to entry for new players. Indeed, the dataBANK demonstrates a strong link between the effectiveness of long-running campaigns and their ability to act as a barrier to entry (see Appendix).

Optrex campaign

The Optrex campaign of 1983–1991 successfully deterred expected new entrants to its category as well as forcing the withdrawal of one existing competitor. Category dominance was strengthened from 84% to 91% market share (see the 1992 case study).

Again, the dataBANK findings agree with the published research. Table 27 shows that small brands need high levels of excess SOV, whereas big brands can get away with less. However, the SOV–SOM levels are higher than those reported by Jones. This is undoubtedly due to the fact that IPA cases cover growing brands, whereas Jones looked at brands in equilibrium.

Table 27: Smaller brands need greater excess SOV to grow

Brand market share (band)	Average SOV–SOM recorded
0–5%	14.6%
6–10%	10.3%
11–20%	13.5%
21–30%	3.9%
>30%	−2.0%

Table 27 shows that **small brands need higher levels of excess SOV** to achieve growth than big brands do. This is not because small brands are unresponsive to advertising. Far from it. In fact, the dataBANK shows that **small brands are more responsive to advertising** than big ones. We will return to this in Part 7, but the effect can be seen here in Figure 17, which shows that increasing the level of SOV makes far more difference to the rate of growth for a small brand than it does for a big one.

However, **big brands gain more growth from non-advertising factors**. This explains why the growth rates for big brands in Figure 17 are always higher than those for small brands, regardless of SOV. As a result of these non-advertising factors, **big brands tend to outperform small ones** at all but the very highest level of SOV.

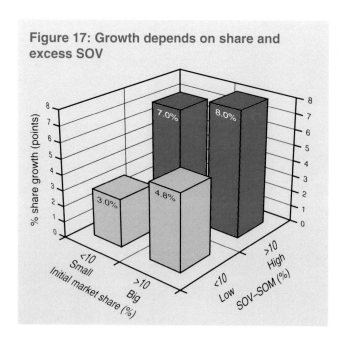

Figure 17: Growth depends on share and excess SOV

Other factors can also affect required budget

Clearly, the correlation curve is a best fit – in a sense, what the average brand of a given size might expect. For those who don't believe in averages, or who like to buck the rules, it is interesting to examine the cases that deviated from the curve significantly.

- Those that lie more than 10% above the curve are mostly launches or relaunches where extensive change to the marketing mix occurred. **If there is a lot of news, brands can create greater sales effects for the same budget** or alternatively spend less for the same effect. This is consistent with communications that are working at both high- and low-attention processing, generating strong short- and long-term sales effects.

- Those that lie more than 10% below the curve are mostly brands in categories with a strong own-label presence. **Own-label products can often capture a significant share of the market without being explicitly advertised, and this changes the SOM–SOV relationship.** It also means that a major task of campaigns is likely to be to justify a price premium; thus a significant profit effect may be achieved without significant share growth. If your brand operates in such a market, one solution for budgeting may be to look at the relationship between SOV and branded market share.

It is also interesting to look at how the SOV–SOM vs growth line changes as categories age through the life cycle. It is unsurprising to find that **greater growth is achieved in younger, growing categories for a given SOV–SOM level** than in older, mature or declining categories. Typically younger categories are less crowded with brands and, with growth for all, competitor response to successful marketing is often less vicious. Launches are also more common in younger categories, and in general there is usually more news for advertising to talk about. Mature categories, on the other hand, tend to be less differentiated and to have a stronger own-label presence, making it tougher to gain market share through advertising. This is particularly true of fmcg categories, which tend to be less responsive to SOV than categories such as services or durables, which are generally less dominated by own label.

This life cycle effect is quite considerable – new and growing categories are almost three times as responsive to advertising as mature and declining ones. However, set against this is the likelihood that in growing categories total communications expenditure will be higher as a proportion of sales than in mature and declining categories, so it may cost more to achieve equilibrium SOV in growing categories (all other factors being equal).

There is also some evidence that **excess SOV produces stronger growth when markets are buoyant** than when they are depressed. This makes sense: consumers probably pay more attention to factors such as price when times are tough. However, this does not necessarily mean that manufacturers should cut budgets when faced with recession. Because media prices tend to fall, the cost of buying a given level of share of voice may be lower when times are tough. In fact, various studies (e.g. Biel & King 1999) suggest that brands that maintain SOV during recession tend to do better than their rivals in the long run.

In Part 7, further evidence will be presented to demonstrate that brands are more responsive to advertising when:

- the brand is new
- the brand is small
- the category is young
- the market is buoyant.

There may well be other factors that affect the responsiveness of individual markets. For instance, the DDB study of Durables category B (a B2B market) referred to in Table 26, showed that this category was much less responsive to advertising than average. If possible, **it is therefore recommended that the SOV–SOM relationship for a particular market be measured before setting budgets**.

Treat non-advertising share of voice in the same way

Although the analysis above is principally (but not universally) based on advertising share of voice, the same principles should apply to non-advertising channels, so long as consistent expenditure data are available. Getting accurate competitive data is still often a problem for non-advertising channels, but as this improves the SOV method should be used to set budgets across the whole range of channels.

Define your category carefully when measuring share of voice and share of market

One final question is left unanswered by the above: what if the brand is the category, or so completely dominates it that notions of SOV and SOM are meaningless? In some instances, it will be possible to take a wider view of the category that includes significant competitors in other subcategories that meet broadly similar consumer needs. Using this broader category definition should ensure that defection between subcategories is controlled. Otherwise, the only basis for budget setting will be category-growth related and is likely to require econometric modelling to determine the optimum marketing mix for growth.

Other methods of budget setting

Broadbent (1989) lists a number of ways in which budgets are commonly set. The main methods are reviewed below:

1. *Advertising to sales ratio*: budgets are set at a fixed ratio to anticipated sales, usually based on the average ratio for the category and a multiple of the previous year's sales. This method takes no account of the earlier observation that large brands can prosper with smaller relative spends than small brands. Perhaps more worryingly, the method can result in under-investment leading to even greater under-investment if A/S ratios are set too low, sparking a spiral of decline for the brand. This is because marketing leads sales, not vice versa, so allowing past sales to determine marketing budgets is an inherently unstable system. Profit impacts are not built into the method.

2. *Advertising to margin ratio*: budgets are set at a fixed ratio of anticipated profit. This suffers from all the same drawbacks of the previous method, except that at least some relationship to profitability is in-built.

3. *Inflation multiplier*: budgets are set relative to the previous year's budget, the relationship determined typically by media inflation (or some other multiple). This method at least aims to achieve stable share of voice, or more precisely stable impacts (although since no account is taken of competitive activity, SOV is likely to be imprecise). Many of the same reservations apply here as to earlier methods.

4. *Affordability*: budgets are set by elimination – what is left over after other calls on sales revenue have been met. This is perhaps the most insensitive method, in which no account has been taken of sales/profits or potential sales/profits. It can be dangerous in the hands of short-term profit seekers because there is no control on sustainability of sales.

5. *Area testing*: budgets are set through experimentation with different levels in different areas to see which level optimises margin. This method is potentially very precise, if properly monitored and evaluated, but there are many variables to take account of and econometric modelling is likely to be essential. It clearly requires considerable time to test and evaluate, but may be worth it: there are many examples of successful use by IPA cases, but the challenges of doing so are discussed in Part 6.

6. *Matching competitors*: budgets are set by reference to key competitors' spend. This method is potentially insensitive to the differences between brands and their communications: it is unlikely that simple matching is optimal, but what differences should be applied? It assumes that competitors have optimised their budgets, which may not be the case, and the consequences of a number of competitors using budget matching are not likely to help profits.

7. *Modelling*: budgets are set following modelling of the historic or regional sales effect of varying budget (SOV) levels. If profit data is included in the model, it can be used to predict the optimum future budget for maximum profit return and has the potential therefore to be an extremely powerful business tool. However, modelling is an expert process requiring much data and time. The outputs of the model will only be as good as the modelling and data on which it is based.

Summary: golden rules for budget setting

1. Level of budget is an extremely powerful determinant of scale of outcomes, so it is essential for accountability that results are set in the context of expenditure.

2. Category share of voice, rather than budget size, most accurately predicts success, and therefore some view of likely competitive expenditure must be factored into budgeting.

3. Advertising-to-sales ratios (a common budget-setting metric) are unreliable for setting budgets because they implicitly assume a linear relationship between brand size and scale of effect. In general, small brands need higher A/S ratios than big ones.

4. It is 'excess' SOV (SOV minus SOM) that most closely determines effects, so make this the KPI. Calculate SOM by value, if possible.

5. Monitor value share growth in relation to excess SOV – specifically, is the campaign performing above the correlation curve or below it, given its size and the life-stage of the category?

6. For an 'average' campaign for an 'average' brand, expect market share growth of about one percentage point per year for each 10 percentage points of 'excess' SOV.

7. However, faster growth can be expected for bigger brands (economies of scale) and launches (new news). Newer and more buoyant categories are also more responsive.

8. If possible, measure the specific relationship between SOV and SOM for your specific category so that you have an accurate benchmark for your brand.

9. If possible, extend the SOV analysis to include non-advertising channels.

10. If available, econometrics is probably the most accurate method for setting budgets. Other methods, such as area testing, are helpful too. However, when such methods are unavailable, the share of voice (SOV) method is extremely useful.

11. If your brand appears to dominate its category, try using a wider category definition; SOV analysis may still be useful. Otherwise, use other methods, such as econometrics.

12. If own label has a significant presence in your category, consider excluding own label when calculating SOM.

4 Communications strategy

Part 2 has already touched on communications strategy, in so far as objectives sometimes imply certain communications strategies. However, this is less precise than looking at the model of consumer influence used. So in this section, the detailed patterns of effectiveness resulting from the various communications models will be examined to provide guidance on what to expect – and therefore measure – from different approaches and different market situations.

Models of consumer influence

In terms of the communications influence model adopted, the data classify campaigns in six ways (see Table 28). The overall frequency of the various influence models in the dataBANK is also shown. The definitions are the ones provided to case study authors, and are based on familiar influence models in use by leading market research companies. For greater clarity, further observations on the practical interpretation of each model follow below.

Table 28: Classification of campaigns

Influence model	Definition of how the campaign worked	Exemplar	Frequency (%)
Emotional involvement	Simply because of the emotions or feelings the campaign touched/how likeable it was	Honda	23%
Fame	Got the brand talked about/made it famous	118 118	9%
Information	Simply because of the information the campaign provided	No More Nails	10%
Persuasion	Initially gained interest with information, then added emotional appeal	Tesco	29%
Reinforcement	Reinforced existing behaviour rather than changed behaviour (the weak theory)	BT call stimulation	3%
More complex	A more complex combination of these or other factors	O$_2$	25%

'Emotional involvement' campaigns work by touching emotions or feelings in consumers and/or by being well liked *per se*: they generate emotional engagement with the campaign. The intention is to transfer these emotions to the brand and consequently to build empathy in the consumer–brand relationship. Through empathy they seek to influence choice. In practice these campaigns do sometimes include information about the brand, but it is judged secondary or inconsequential to the success of the campaign.

'Fame' campaigns work by getting the brand talked about and generally making it more famous. This is not the same as saying the advertising is designed to raise brand awareness (which most advertising seeks to do) – it is about creating perceptions of being the brand that is 'making waves'. These campaigns often generate strong emotional responses in the target group (not necessarily liking) and so cause the brand to stand out distinctly from other brands in the category. They usually become talked about not in a functional way, but by virtue of the attitudes and point of view they project for the brand. Prue (1998) has reported that this encourages brand usage by creating perceptions that the brand is bigger and more 'important' than before.

'Information' campaigns work simply by providing information relating to the brand. In practice information can be about the brand, the category, the user or their world. These campaigns do not attempt to use emotional 'tools' to influence consumers. As well as a number of not-for-profit government information campaigns, this category also includes classic 'reason why' advertising, in which a functional product benefit over competing brands is communicated (such as 'works fastest', or more often these days 'no other brand works faster'). The essential characteristic of 'information' campaigns is that they present a purely logical rationale for usage or trial.

'Persuasion' campaigns work by initially gaining the interest of consumers with information or news, but then adding an emotional element to help persuade and/or make the message more memorable. The information often seeks to challenge or enhance existing knowledge or beliefs about the brand. In practice, the emotional content is often quite low-key and the process of persuasion to use or try is essentially rational.

'Reinforcement' campaigns seek to reinforce existing behaviour rather than change behaviour. In doing so they are in part aiming to increase loyalty through increased frequency and weight of brand usage. These campaigns typically reinforce particular behaviours such as usage occasions or usage modes, or strengthen the linkage between usage and associated events (e.g. telephone call stimulation).

'More complex' campaigns work by a combination of two or more of the other five modi operandi, or very occasionally in ways that fall outside this. The overlapping modes included in the 'more complex' cases are revealed in Table 29.

Table 29

Constituent influence modes of 'More complex' campaigns	Incidence among 'More complex' campaigns
Emotional involvement	76%
Fame	33%
Information	49%
Persuasion	52%
Reinforcement	7%

Analysing the mix of these constituent modes demonstrates that in practice the key characteristic of 'more complex' cases is the combination of rational and emotional platforms in comparatively equal measure (see Table 30).

Table 30

Nature of influence of 'More complex' cases	Incidence among 'More complex' cases
Principally emotional	17%
Emotional and rational	71%
Principally rational	12%

The majority of the more complex cases (60%) comprise emotional involvement coupled with the more rational approaches of either information or rational persuasion. Arguably, these two

The British Airways twin-track campaign

An illustration of both the twin-strand approach and the multiple-mode approach can be found in the twin-track British Airways campaign of 2004. One campaign track redefined some of the 'frills' of the service as *important* (e.g. reserved seats and proximity of airports to city centres) by playing on the emotional disappointments of new low-cost airline services. The other track simultaneously evoked the reassuring experiential and emotional values, inherent after long use, of the Delibes 'Lakmé' music track, while communicating a rational low-cost message (evidenced by sample fares).

combinations are not importantly different. Authors appear to categorise cases as the former where the information content is intended to be a statement of fact rather than a comparative claim. In some 'more complex' cases different elements (often media) of the campaign employ a different mode, such as breakfast cereal campaigns that include two strands appealing differently to parents and their kids. They also include cases where individual executions employ multiple modes. So, one way or another, 'more complex' cases tend to mix emotional and rational approaches and, as will be shown, these cases tend to work in a way that is halfway between the two.

Not all influence models are equally powerful

Although the patterns of usage suggest, as before, that most communications models can work in most situations, the data reveal that some models work better than others (see Table 31).

Table 31: Emotionally-based influence models are more effective

	Influence model					
	Fame	Emotional involvement	More complex	Persuasion	Information	Reinforcement
Effectiveness success rate	72%	68%	68%	61%	61%	33% (– –)
Accountability success rate	76%	73%	61% (– –)	76%	74%	55%

The broad conclusion from the data is that **communications models that use emotional appeal (emotional involvement, fame and 'more complex' models) are more likely to yield strong business results than rationally based models (information and persuasion)**. This is in line with much historic research on the power of emotional approaches (see Feldwick and Heath 2007 for a review). The differences become even more apparent when the detailed pattern of effects is examined (see Table 32).

Emotionally based campaigns are not only more likely to produce very large business effects but also produce more of them, outperforming rationally based campaigns on every single business measure. In particular, they are significantly more profitable than rational campaigns. This is especially true of 'fame' campaigns, whose superior potency is also due in part to their impact on price sensitivity. This is consistent with the finding of Part 2 (Table 7) that campaigns that target more effects are more profitable.

Table 32: Emotional campaigns generate more business effects

reporting very large effects on:	Influence model*				
	Fame	Emotional involvement	'More complex'	Persuasion	Information
Sales	58%	57% (+)	45%	46%	48%
Market share	31%	35%	31%	27%	27%
Profit	39% (++)	28%	26%	13% (– –)	24%
Penetration	33%	24%	35% (+)	25%	24%
Loyalty	11%	9%	9%	7%	3%
Price sensitivity	8%	2%	7%	3%	0%
Any measure	72%	68%	68%	61%	61%
Average number of v large effects	**1.8**	**1.6**	**1.5**	**1.2**	**1.3**

*NB: Reinforcement model excluded because of small sample size

It is worth dwelling on the merits of fame campaigns because they benefit from a 'double whammy' of greater effectiveness and greater accountability (since 'fame' is quite readily measurable). As a strategic approach they therefore offer a solution to some of the tensions between accountability and effectiveness.

Reinforcement campaigns are too few in number to form detailed conclusions about, but are generally the weakest of all (95% confidence), which is consistent with what has already been said in Part 2 about the difficulty of successfully increasing loyalty. The net result of this is that **reinforcement campaigns are the least profitable of all**.

Emotionally based campaigns build key consumer attitudes more powerfully

It has been shown that emotionally based campaigns bring greater business effects, notably bigger profit gains. Table 33 demonstrates that the same is true of intermediate effects: in general emotionally based campaigns generate more numerous intermediate effects. It will be shown in Part 6 that business

Table 33: Emotionally based campaigns generate more numerous intermediate effects

reporting very large effects on:	Influence model*				
	Fame	Emotional involvement	More complex	Persuasion	Information
Brand awareness	58% (+++)	35%	30%	33%	41%
Brand commitment	13%	22% (++)	17%	6% (– –)	9%
Brand fame	53% (+++)	15%	22%	10% (– –)	16%
Brand differentiation	29%	24%	24%	12% (– –)	13%
Quality perceptions	8%	16%	18%	9%	16%
Brand image	18%	17%	31% (+++)	8% (– – –)	25%
Brand trust	0% (–)	4%	14% (+++)	2%	9%
Average number of v large effects	**2.2**	**1.6**	**2.0**	**1.2**	**1.7**

The power of emotional campaigns

Two case studies illustrate the greater effectiveness of emotionally based campaigns over rationally based ones *comparatively*: Cravendale and Tropicana.

The original Cravendale campaign

The subsequent campaign

The original Cravendale Milk launch campaign was an informational one, extolling the benefits and features of the milk. When it failed to meet business targets it was replaced by an emotional campaign, 'The Cows Want it Back', celebrating the implied quality of the product. Business targets were surpassed.

The original Tropicana campaign

The subsequent campaign

The Tropicana fruit juice campaign illustrates the relative power of a fame communications strategy over a rational persuasion one. An earlier campaign extolled the natural, unprocessed benefits of the brand, but failed to arrest continuing share decline, despite a well-liked and highly memorable execution. Replacement by a fame strategy in which the brand was associated with New York breakfasts (the perceived gold standard of the art of fine breakfasting), accompanied by a popular synergistic music track revival, brought about an immediate reversal of the share decline and a healthy return on investment.

effectiveness correlates closely with the *number* of very large intermediate effects observed, so it is no coincidence that emotional campaigns are more prolific.

The data also give an insight into how emotional campaigns work. **Emotional campaigns outperform rational ones on almost every single attitudinal dimension.** They are better at generating awareness and commitment. But, more importantly, they are very much better at creating authority (fame) for brands and at differentiating them – and in the case of more complex campaigns, at raising quality perceptions. These three intermediate effects appear to represent a 'holy trinity' of profitability.

The relative strength of emotional campaigns' ability to build brand differentiation over rational campaigns is important and revealing. It illustrates not only the practical difficulties of differentiating brands by rational means in a world where functional brand advantages are rare and short-lived, but also that merely stating the rational basis of brand differentiation is insufficient. To be accepted and remembered most powerfully, a brand difference must be emotionally engaging to the consumer. There are many fine examples of this in the dataBANK, but perhaps two recent ones illustrate the point well: O_2 and Marks & Spencer.

The power of emotional campaigns to differentiate

The success of O$_2$ in marketing terms has been built on an emotional platform of being a consumer champion in a category of technology-led brands whose key focus was to sell network capacity to consumers. A very different brand was created with a different consumer-led language and tone; although marketing products that were usually only fleetingly differentiated, the brand has become powerfully emotionally differentiated and hugely more profitable.

After many false starts at renaissance, the troubled M&S brand finally convinced customers to return to the aisles with a campaign that relied heavily on the emotional appeal of pure showmanship – 'fame' in the terminology of the dataBANK– rather than rational product messaging.

Emotionally based campaigns are more memorable

Implicit within the above is another widely accepted advantage of emotionally based campaigns – namely their stronger impact on memory formation. It is likely that the greater ability of emotional communications to form durable memories of the brand in the minds of consumers plays a major role in their commercial success. The issue of brand saliency is revisited in Part 6, but some interesting light is shed on the role of memorability in the effectiveness of emotional campaigns by another finding of the dataBANK. **Rational campaigns are more effective (albeit by a small margin) in directly influencing consumer behaviour** – that is, short-term behavioural responses such as those sought by conventional direct-response campaigns (see Table 34).

Table 34: Rational campaigns are better at (short-term) direct influence of consumers

	Influence model*				
	Fame	Emotional involvement	More complex	Persuasion	Information
% campaigns reporting very large direct effects	32%	27%	31%	33%	41%

Such effects do not in general require long-term memory formation: the required consumer behaviour is either immediate (e.g. call the number or visit the website) or short order (e.g. try new uses for a familiar product). Once the event has been triggered, it matters little that the stimulus is forgotten – a sequence of events has begun. Only on this short-term effectiveness measure do rationally based campaigns outperform others.

Emotionally based influence models deserve to be more widespread

The frequency of use of the various models in the dataBANK (see Table 28) does not generally reflect their relative levels of effectiveness. Rational persuasion is the most widely used model, yet one of the least effective. Fame is the most effective model overall, yet it is the second least widely used. Only the reinforcement model appears to deserve its level of popularity – used in only 3% of cases.

Accountability helps to explain the popularity of the persuasion model (although there are other cultural reasons – see Feldwick and Heath 2007). Despite mediocre business results, campaigns that work on the persuasion model have one of the highest success rates in the IPA Awards, suggesting that causality is easy to prove for such cases. Once again the results in Part 6 corroborate this finding: it will be shown that campaigns that get high persuasion scores tend to perform particularly well on intermediate measures, although not in terms of business effects.

So marketers face a dilemma. **Emotional campaigns are highly effective, but difficult to measure in tracking research. Rational campaigns track well, making them more accountable, but don't deliver such good business results**.

The fame model is one solution to this dilemma. Fame campaigns are the most effective overall in business terms, performing particularly well in terms of profitability. Yet they are also highly accountable, with one of the highest success rates in the Awards. In Part 6, it will become clear why this is – when a brand becomes famous, *all* the intermediate metrics tend to improve, making fame campaigns fairly easy to track.

The data thus argue strongly for the more widespread adoption of fame as an influence model – not only is it more effective but also highly accountable, because the desired effect of brand authority is quite readily measurable.

Different strategies for different contexts

Thus far, generalisations have been made about the effectiveness of different strategic communications models, but what about their effectiveness in specific contexts? This section reports any meaningful deviations from the general patterns reported above.

Emotional campaigns win out even in rational categories

In categories where brand choice is predominantly an emotional decision, emotional campaigns are, unsurprisingly, more effective than rational campaigns. However, the reverse is not true: in categories defined by rational brand evaluation, emotional campaigns remain more effective, although their advantage over rational campaigns is smaller (see Table 35).

This supports the hypothesis that emotional campaigns exert greater influence on brand choice and/or are more memorable than rational campaigns; one way or another, the cumulative effect of emotional campaigns over time is greater than that of rational campaigns.

Table 35: Effectiveness of influence models in rational vs emotional categories

	Influence models		
Effectiveness success rate:	Fame + Emotional involvement	More complex	Persuasion + Information
Predominantly emotional purchase decision	78%	72%	55% (−)
Predominantly rational purchase decision	75%	44% (−)	67%

Premium brands need emotional support

It is perhaps not surprising that emotional campaigns are more effective for premium brands, given that rational messages concerned with price are likely to be less relevant. But the scale of the difference between the effectiveness of emotional and rational campaigns for premium brands suggests that more is at play here. Premium brands appear to *need* the support of emotional attributes more acutely than non-premium brands to justify their premium position in the category (see Table 36).

Table 36: Effectiveness of influence models for premium vs non-premium brands

	Influence models		
Effectiveness success rate:	Fame + Emotional involvement	More complex	Persuasion + Information
Value + mid-market brands	66%	76%	72%
Premium + super-premium brands	80%	75%	64%

This is reflected in the predominance of emotional decision making for premium brands (see Table 37).

Table 37: Emotional brand choice dominates premium segments

	Price segments	
Nature of decision making within market segments:	Value + mid-market segments	Premium + super-premium segments
Predominantly emotional purchase decision	37%	50%
Equally emotional and rational	40%	34%
Predominantly rational purchase decision	23%	16%

Emotional campaigns work best during buoyant times

As a partial corollary to the last point, emotional campaigns become relatively more effective in buoyant market conditions, when consumers are perhaps less focused on price and value messages. Tough times seem to demand a more complex approach, mixing emotional and rational tactics (e.g. mixing brand messages with price or promotional messages), see Table 38.

Table 38: Effectiveness of influence models in buoyant and tough times

Effectiveness success rate:	Influence models		
	Fame + Emotional involvement	More complex	Persuasion + Information
High/medium growth	78%	72%	72%
Low growth, stagnant or declining	68%	74%	63%

Emotions become more important as categories mature

The efficiency of emotional brand messaging also becomes more important in mature and, especially, in declining categories. Such categories tend to be characterised by low functional differentiation and narrow profit margins (which reduce the scope for competing on price). It is therefore likely that, in these categories, brand growth is more likely to be fuelled by emotional messaging (see Table 39).

Table 39: Effectiveness of influence models in various category life-stages

Effectiveness success rate:	Influence models		
	Fame + Emotional involvement	More complex	Persuasion + Information
New/growth categories	76%	83%	71%
Mature categories	71%	69%	65%
Declining categories	56%	58%	33%

Set against this, Table 39 demonstrates that the relative power of rational campaigns rises in new and growth categories, where perhaps there is important news to be communicated. But the evidence as a whole suggests that, even in nascent categories, wise marketers will be building enduring emotional brand equities to see them through the swiftly approaching days of cut-throat competition: one need look no further than the iPod to see the benefits of this approach played out. Leaving potent emotional territory free for a future challenger looks increasingly like recklessness.

Emotions and fame work best for smaller brands

Brand size influences the relative effectiveness of the strategic models in a number of ways. Emotional involvement is effective for most brands, but becomes particularly important for smaller ones. On the other hand, brand leaders are one group that actually benefit from a more rational approach, presumably because (as was discussed in Part 3) economies of scale give them more advantages in terms of product and price that they can talk about (see Table 40).

This echoes strongly a central theme of Morgan (2000) concerning the importance of emotionally engaging 'lighthouse identities' for successful challenger brands fighting against the brand leader's economies of scale and 'double jeopardy'. This is especially the case in categories dominated by emotional decision making, where brand saliency is more likely to be fuelled by emotional messaging.

Table 40: Effectiveness of 'Emotional involvement' for challenger brands

Effectiveness success rate:	Influence model'	
	'Emotional involvement'	Average of all models
Niche and small brands	82%	73%
Strong challenger brands	71%	67%
Leader brands	47%	61%

Looking at the different types of emotional approach, the particular strength of the fame model is revealed to be in the domain of smaller brands – it is of average effectiveness for larger brands, but considerably above average for smaller brands (see Table 41).

Table 41: Effectiveness of 'Fame' for small vs large brands

Effectiveness success rate:	Influence model	
	'Fame'	Average of all models
Small brands	90%	72%
Large brands	65%	64%

Rational approaches work best for direct response

It was shown earlier (Table 34) that direct behavioural response is one area where rational approaches seem to be more effective than emotional ones.

This may not only be as a result of direct response requiring just a short-term effect, where the superior memorability of emotional messages carries no particular advantage. It may also be a result of direct activity tending to target consumers who are actively shopping for a product, rather than those who are merely absorbing brand messages in a passive way. Active shoppers tend to demand more detailed information and, as Heath has argued (2001), tend to process that information in a more rational way.

In categories where purchase intervals are long (e.g. durables and some services), consumers tend to alternate between distinct passive and active phases. For such categories, it may be effective to target passive consumers with more emotional brand messages, while using more information-rich channels to influence active shoppers (see box on Volkswagen).

Emotional campaigns win out in all major category types

But what of the 'my category is a special case' belief? The data in Table 42 demonstrates that emotional influence models win out across most major category groupings: fmcg, durables and not-for-profit. Only in services does a mixed approach seem to work better than pure emotion, and this may reflect the fact that the direct relationship with the consumer that many service brands enjoy is particularly suited to direct marketing (which, as has just been shown, tends to be a more rational channel).

The use of rational messages in the Volkswagen campaign

Part of the passive campaign (above)

Part of the active campaign (right)

Volkswagen communications adopted a 'purchase funnel' approach from 1995. This was an example of a 'more complex' campaign, in which different elements of the campaign targeted passive prospects (not yet actively buying) and active prospects (who were currently in the market). An emotive brand message was communicated to the former, while detailed product information was targeted at the latter. Over the next seven years value share doubled, driven in part by more efficient use of the communications budget and enhanced direct response rates.

Table 42: Effectiveness of influence models in various categories

Effectiveness success rate:	Influence models		
	Fame + Emotional involvement	'More Complex'	Persuasion + Information
fmcg categories	73%	70%	67%
Durables	85%	75%	64%
Services	59%	82% (+)	63%
Not-for-profit	17%	38%	0% (−)

So, in general, there is little evidence to support the existence of special case categories in which the general observations about influence models are overturned.

Creative styles are generally similarly effective

If there are significant differences between the effectiveness of different strategic communications approaches, the same cannot be said of creative styles of TV advertising: there are few differences to report (see Figure 18). Sex as a creative tool appears effective, but not significantly more so than other styles. There appears to be no difference between live action and animation, and the use of humour or celebrities appears to do nothing to enhance effectiveness in general. The only style that appears to be less effective, in general, is testimonial. The clear conclusion is to keep an open mind about creative style, pursuing whatever route most powerfully executes the intended strategic direction (see Figure 18).

Figure 18: Creative styles make little difference

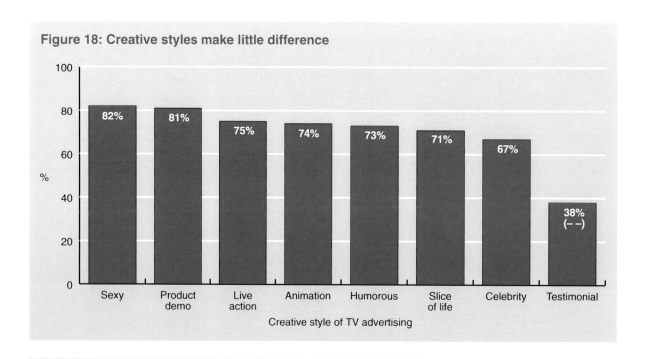

Creative style of TV advertising

Summary: golden rules for communications strategy

1. Aim to change behaviour, rather than merely reinforce existing behaviour. The reinforcement strategy is the least effective of all.

2. Emotional approaches generally work better than rational ones, regardless of category, though the intermediate effects (on brand health) are not always easy to measure.

3. Put emotions at the core of your campaign. Don't just 'bolt on' emotions to a rational proposition (the persuasion model).

4. The fame model is the most effective emotional strategy of all. Making your brand 'famous' in its category can lead to big profit gains, partly because of the effect on price sensitivity. Fame campaigns are also highly accountable (unlike more subtle emotional approaches), since they are quite easy to track.

5. The more emotional the purchase decision, the better emotions work. But, even in very rational categories, emotional approaches tend to work better than rational ones.

6. Emotional approaches work well in mature markets, where they can help to differentiate between essentially similar products. Products in younger markets are more differentiated, favouring a mix of emotions and information.

7. Emotional approaches work particularly well for premium brands as a way of justifying the price premium. Value brands require a more mixed approach.

8. Emotions work best when markets are buoyant. When times are tough, price becomes more important, so use a more mixed approach (e.g. emotive brand message plus price communications).

9. Unlike most brands, market leaders can successfully exploit a more rational approach because they have more product and price advantages to talk about.

10. Direct response requires a more rational approach. But also consider using emotions to 'warm up' consumers before they start actively shopping.

Marketing in the Era of Accountability

5 Media strategy

This part will examine the patterns of media and channel usage that promote effectiveness and will, in particular, probe the effectiveness of TV and how this has changed since the advent of digital media. Implications for new media will also be drawn.

Multi-channel campaigns are more effective

The proliferation of media and communications channels over the 26 years of the IPA Effectiveness Awards is well known and widely reported. So too is the trend for campaigns to make wider use of these communications tools, and this is reflected in the dataBANK, both in terms of the number of advertising media channels used and the broader number of communications channels used (see Figure 19).

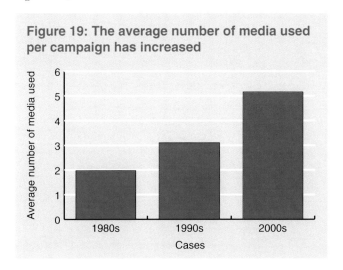

Figure 19: The average number of media used per campaign has increased

Clearly, effectiveness has been aided by the wider choice of channels available and a number of case studies have quantified the multiplier effects of using them synergistically in integrated campaigns (e.g. Lynx, Cravendale, VW Passat).

The dataBANK shows that these multiplier effects are not isolated examples. **Multi-channel campaigns are in general more effective than single-channel campaigns** (see Table 43).

Table 43: The power of multi-channel campaigns

	Single-channel campaigns	Multi-channel campaigns
Effectiveness success rate	58%	65%
Accountability success rate	81% (++)	71%

This is not simply the result of bigger budgets. Repeating the share of voice analysis from Part 3 shows that multi-channel campaigns actually make the same budget work harder (see Table 44).

Table 44: Multi-channel campaigns are more efficient

	Single-channel campaigns	Multi-channel campaigns
Average SOM gain per 10% points excess SOV	1.2%	2.4%

However, it should be noted that, while multi-channel campaigns tend to have bigger effects, single-channel campaigns tend to win more prizes. This is probably due to nothing more than the greater ease of isolating their effects. Once again, there is a tension between accountability and effectiveness. Ironically, **the trend towards integration may actually be making marketing less accountable, not more so.**

Some published multiplier effects

The Lynx (Axe) campaign was 2.25 times more effective in the UK where it was part of an integrated multi-channel campaign, than in France, where it was a single-channel (advertising-only) campaign.

The Cravendale Milk campaign demonstrated the multiplier effects listed in the table.

Cravendale: multiplier effects

Channels used	Sales uplift
TV only	4.9%
DM (door-drop) only	8.6%
Point-of-sale (POS) only	0.5%
TV + DM	31.7%
TV + POS	22.5%

VW Passat: multiplier effects

Channels exposed to	Consumer interest
Advertising only	22%
Advertising + PR	40%
Advertising + DM	42%

The VW Passat campaign demonstrated the multiplier effects listed in the table above, among non-owners.

Sadly, the data do not allow conclusions to be drawn about the different styles of integration used in multi-channel campaigns.

Beware of spreading the advertising budget too thinly

But if integrated multi-channel campaigns are a good thing, then the data suggest that it is possible to have too much of a good thing. While increasing the number of advertising media increases effectiveness at first (regardless of budget), there is a significant 'tailing off' of levels of effectiveness as the number of media increases beyond a certain optimum. **The data suggest that around three advertising media is optimal for a typical campaign** (though clearly this will rise for larger budgets), see Table 45.

Table 45: Average effectiveness levels of different numbers of ATL media					
	1	2	3	4	5
Effectiveness success rate	59%	64%	74% (++)	62%	57%

There are several reasons why adding more media is not always a good idea. First, there are diminishing returns in terms of coverage – after a certain point, adding more media does not give you much more reach. Second, as the number of media used increases, the share of budget that needs to be allocated to production costs increases. Third, spreading a budget across a large number of media may make it harder to cut through in any of them.

The last two of these reasons both suggest that the optimum number of media will increase with budget, and the dataBANK confirms that this is indeed the case. For campaigns with larger budgets (over £4.5 million at 2005 prices), the optimum is around four media, rather than three.

So, although the optimum spread of channels for a given brand will depend in part on the budget available and in part on the nature of the marketing task, marketers should be wary of spreading their advertising budget too thinly across too many media.

TV has become more effective and more efficient

The demise of the 30-second TV spot has been widely forecast, as channel proliferation and viewing levels conspire to make it ever more difficult to reach a mass audience. But the evidence of the dataBANK is that reports of the death of TV are greatly exaggerated.

Looking back over the last 26 years, it is clear that TV has historically been a highly effective medium. **Campaigns that have used TV have significantly outperformed those that have not** (see Figure 20).

This is not merely a budget effect – TV has outperformed other channels, even for small-budget campaigns. Indeed, SOV analysis shows that **using TV makes a campaign much more efficient, regardless of budget** (see Figure 21).

The fact that TV is one of the most effective media is entirely consistent with the findings in Part 4 about influence models. There it was shown that the most effective campaigns are those that rely primarily on emotional rather than rational messages. Film is unarguably the most emotionally rich of the traditional advertising media. So one would expect TV advertising to be more effective. In Part 4, it was shown that fame is a particularly potent way to promote a brand. TV is also unrivalled for its

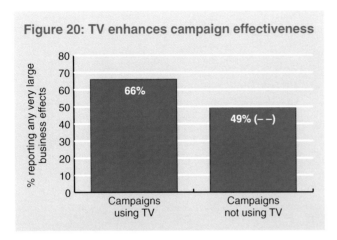

Figure 20: TV enhances campaign effectiveness

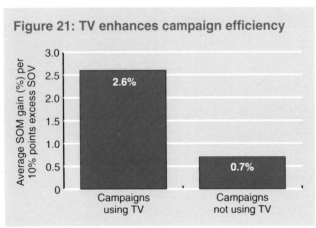

Figure 21: TV enhances campaign efficiency

potential to create a sense of fame around people and events, so once again it is not surprising that it can enhance the effectiveness of campaigns.

A further explanation of the power of TV may be found within Heath's theory of low-attention processing (Heath 2001), which seems to be corroborated by the findings of the IPA dataBANK to some extent (see 'Are campaigns strong or weak forces?' in Part 6). Heath argues that advertising is often more effective when it is processed in a low-involvement way, because this tends to lead consumers to judge messages on an emotional rather than a rational basis. Because of the way people use TV to relax, it is uniquely suited to low-involvement processing, and this may be another reason why it is so effective. More recently Feldwick & Heath (2007) have demonstrated that attention levels to print adverts are two to three times greater than TV adverts, and that this makes press a better medium for information. But they also observe that TV's potency lies in its ability to build *relationships* between brands and consumers: an ability they suggest is far more important to effectiveness – **'decision making is always rooted in the emotions.'**

But what is really surprising is not that TV is effective, but that its effectiveness actually seems to be increasing over time. Figure 22 shows that the effect of TV on market share seemed to increase substantially with the launch of satellite TV in the UK, and has increased further over the last decade.

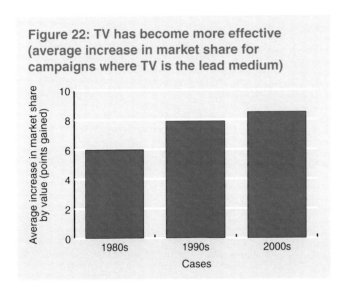

Figure 22: TV has become more effective (average increase in market share for campaigns where TV is the lead medium)

This appears to fly in the face of accepted wisdom about the predicament of TV: declining and fragmenting audiences and spiralling costs. However, closer examination of the data reveals that this view is misinformed.

It is widely assumed that TV viewing is in serious decline in the UK. In fact, after allowing for recorded viewing and new digital multi-channel viewing, it becomes apparent that **total TV viewing has not changed at all over the last 20 years or so** (see Figure 23).

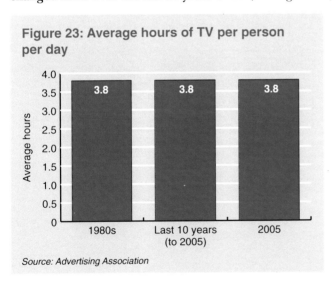

Figure 23: Average hours of TV per person per day

Source: Advertising Association

Moreover, as the number of commercial channels has increased, BBC's share of the total audience has fallen; so **commercial TV viewing has actually risen** (see Figure 24). As a result, taking the medium as a whole, it's actually getting easier to reach people with TV ads, not harder.

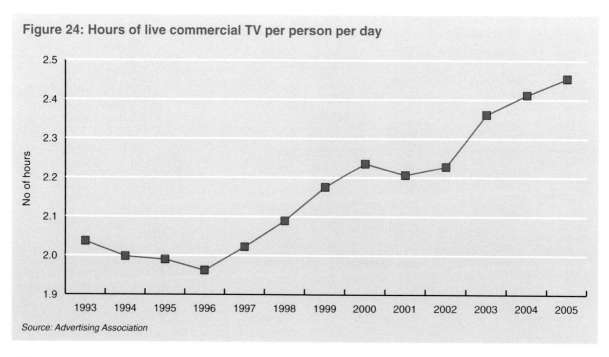

Figure 24: Hours of live commercial TV per person per day

No of hours

Source: Advertising Association

Of course, the proliferation of channels means that the audience for each individual TV spot has shrunk. But spot prices have fallen too. In fact, with more TV spots available, and more TV companies competing against one another, spot prices have fallen faster than audiences. The result is that **the cost of reaching a given audience has actually fallen substantially.** Figure 25 shows that the real average cost per thousand has fallen by 32% since the 1980s, and is currently at its lowest for 25 years.

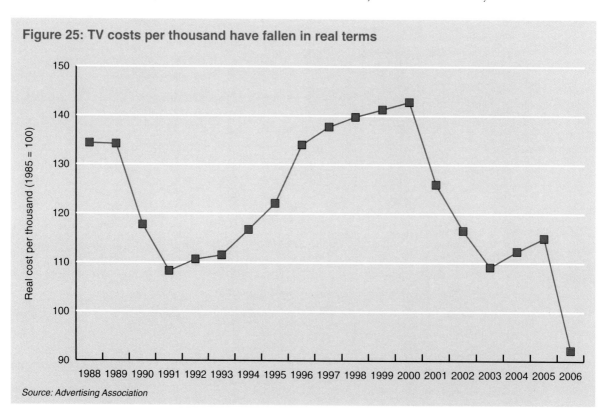

Figure 25: TV costs per thousand have fallen in real terms

Real cost per thousand (1985 = 100)

Source: Advertising Association

Marketing in the Era of Accountability

So, a given TV budget goes about 32% further now than it did in the 1980s. Not only that, but audience fragmentation also allows advertisers to use TV in a more targeted way. One would therefore expect the effectiveness of TV to have increased by more than 32%. Sure enough, **the dataBANK suggests that TV is about 42% more effective now than it was in the 1980s**.

Unpublished econometric analyses undertaken by DDB confirm that TV remains a highly effective medium. There is certainly no econometric evidence that TV is becoming less effective.

It is, of course, possible that this may all change in the future. New technology may eventually make conventional broadcast TV advertising redundant. However, there is no sign of that happening yet in the UK, or indeed the US (where TV viewing is actually increasing).

Felix: an example of the growing power of TV

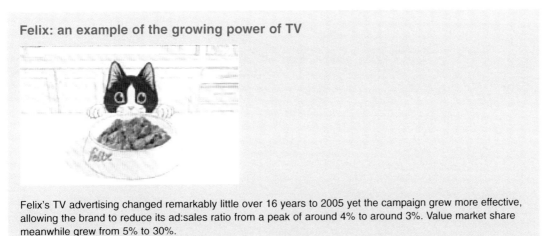

Felix's TV advertising changed remarkably little over 16 years to 2005 yet the campaign grew more effective, allowing the brand to reduce its ad:sales ratio from a peak of around 4% to around 3%. Value market share meanwhile grew from 5% to 30%.

Outdoor is best used as a secondary medium

Unfortunately, there are too few cases in the dataBANK where radio or cinema took the lead to draw many conclusions about the effectiveness of those media (what little data there are suggest they are probably highly effective as well). However, it is clear from the data that **outdoor seems to be generally less effective than TV, at least when it takes the lead**. The apparently lower effectiveness success rate of press as a lead medium is probably simply due to lower budget levels for such campaigns (the disparity is not significant and reduces further when only smaller-budget campaigns are examined). However, this is not the case with outdoor: even with smaller-budget campaigns, outdoor as a lead medium produces fewer very large business effects. Given our findings on the importance of emotion, this is exactly what you would expect for this generally less emotive medium (see Figure 26).

These results do not mean that advertisers should not use outdoor media. On the contrary, the IPA data show that adding them to the mix increases effectiveness. But unless they can be used in a powerfully emotive way (as Wonderbra did), they are generally more suitable as secondary media, rather than primary ones.

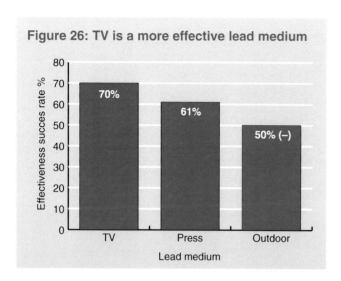

Figure 26: TV is a more effective lead medium

Don't just rely on advertising – use other channels as well

It has already been shown that multi-channel campaigns are more effective than single-channel ones. In particular, the data show that campaigns that supplement advertising with other channels do slightly better than those that rely on advertising alone (see Table 46).

Table 46: Multi-channel campaigns are more effective

	Channels used		
	Traditional advertising alone	Advertising plus other channels	Other channels alone
Frequency	51%	48%	1%
Effectiveness success rate	62%	65%	33%

This effect becomes clearer when the relationship between market share and share of voice is examined. **Campaigns that mix advertising with other channels generate significantly faster growth for the same share of voice** (see Table 47).

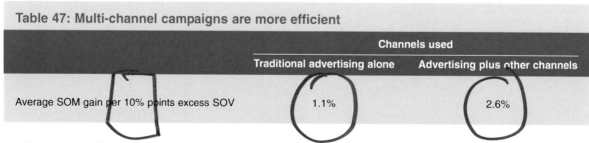

Table 47: Multi-channel campaigns are more efficient

	Channels used	
	Traditional advertising alone	Advertising plus other channels
Average SOM gain per 10% points excess SOV	1.1%	2.6%

As discussed earlier, the data suggest that there are diminishing returns as the number of advertising media increases. However, the same is not true of below-the-line channels, for which it appears to be a case of the more the merrier (provided the budget is big enough) (see Table 48).

Table 48: Effectiveness rises with the number of BTL channels

	1	2	3	4+
Effectiveness success rate	55% (−)	65%	59%	80% (++)

A possible explanation for this is that non-advertising channels are able to perform quite different tasks, whereas extra advertising media tend to compete with each other to perform the same task.

Implications for new media

The IPA dataBANK suggests that the continuing effectiveness of TV is due to the emotive power it can impart to advertising (and possibly to its greater capacity to benefit from low-attention processing), and that the relative effectiveness of other established media broadly reflects their potency in this respect. Since this is founded on the way the human brain processes and stores impressions, there is every reason to believe that the power of new media will be subject to the same criteria. Clearly, some new media operate in the 'direct response' domain where lasting impressions are not required for business effects; but brands cannot be built in this way. The ability of any new medium to replace TV in the engine room of enduring brand profitability will depend on its ability to similarly engage the emotions of consumers. Although great strides in this respect are being made by progressive web developments (most obviously YouTube), the data suggest that, for the time being at least, 'TV' (delivered by whatever channel) remains king.

Summary: golden rules for media strategy

1. Integrated multi-media campaigns work better than single-channel ones (although evaluation is more difficult).

2. However, that doesn't necessarily mean 'surround sound' advertising. Three or four advertising channels (depending on budget) are generally optimal. Beyond that, diminishing returns set in.

3. Don't just rely on advertising – supplement it with other channels. The more non-advertising channels the better, if you can afford them.

4. Don't neglect TV. Far from being dead, TV advertising remains one of the most effective and efficient media. New technology and increased competition may actually be making TV more efficient, not less so.

5. Print media are a useful addition to the mix, but should be used as secondary media in most cases.

6. If longer-term brand effects are an objective, as opposed to short-term response, judge all media opportunities on their power to enhance the ability of communications to engage emotionally with consumers.

6 Measurement

This part will seek to demonstrate which approaches to the measurement of marketing effects are most accountable (i.e. are most convincing), as well as those that promote effectiveness most strongly (i.e. are most linked to business success). In doing so, it will review the theories of communications effects that have shaped contemporary practice – in particular the 'strong' and 'weak' theories, and high- and low-involvement processing.

Hard measures are best

It was stated at the outset of Part 2 that effectiveness is defined essentially as achieving goals. It was also shown that those goals should be prioritised: business objectives come first, closely followed by behavioural objectives, with attitudinal objectives coming third in importance. The importance of evaluation measures should therefore reflect this hierarchy.

Yet a great deal of everyday evaluation appears to place unwarranted importance on intermediate attitudinal measures. This appears to go way beyond the use of intermediate measures as useful leading indicators: too often they become primary objectives *per se*. The dataBANK argues that, when choosing which evaluation measures to use and pay attention to, hard measures should always come first, and the harder the better. So this part will follow the hierarchical pattern established in Part 2, starting with business effects.

Use econometrics to measure financial payback

In Part 2, it was argued that profit should be the ultimate objective for all commercial brands, and that focusing on profit growth leads to more effective communications. **Measures of financial return are, therefore, the ultimate evaluation measures for all commercial campaigns**. Even when the organisation is not a profit-making firm, thinking in terms of the financial value of the effects of marketing can sometimes help (see box on the next page).

Part 7 will explore the measurement of profit return in more detail, but whatever profit metric is chosen, the problem of isolating the contribution of communication will always remain. Econometric modelling is undoubtedly the most reliable method to use here.

The dramatic impact of econometric modelling on effectiveness and accountability was demonstrated in Part 2 (Table 10). **By disentangling the myriad factors that affect sales, econometrics allows accurate measurement of marketing effects**. In particular, econometrics enables the reliable calculation and monitoring of profit returns resulting from marketing, as well as the measurement of price elasticity. Not only that, but the data in Part 2 suggest that **using econometrics on an ongoing basis actually increases effectiveness**, by providing brand management with the information needed to operate all the levers of profitability *optimally*. The benefits and demands of econometric modelling are reviewed by Cook & Holmes (2004).

Yet only 15% of cases in the dataBANK used econometric modelling to identify the effects due to the campaign, and it is likely that the percentage of all brands that use it is lower still. At a stroke, the widespread adoption of econometric modelling as a standard brand management tool would go a long way to addressing the criticisms of marketing identified in Part 2, as well as making a significant impact on profitability.

The use of financial measures in not-for-profit cases

The 1998–2005 Training & Development Agency school teacher recruitment campaign was evaluated in terms of the savings in supply teacher costs brought about by improved recruitment (£4.9bn), as well as the savings in salary costs that would have been incurred to recruit teachers by purely financial rewards (£11.5bn). Set against a £57m communications budget, the return was attractive.

The 1996/7 HEA drugs education campaign evaluated the benefits of reduced drug taking in terms of increased spending on legal purchases that would yield revenue to the treasury (£28m p.a.), as well as the reduced cost of days lost to employers (£11m p.a.).

What if econometric modelling is not possible?

If the means or the data are simply not available for econometric modelling then there are a number of less precise approaches that can be used to establish the effectiveness of campaigns. However, the dataBANK shows that none of them is as successful as econometrics in promoting effectiveness or accountability (Table 49).

Table 49: Relative strengths of analytical approaches

	Method used to establish effectiveness			
	Econometric modelling	User profile/product mix changed in line with strategy	Usage and attitudes changed in line with exposure	Usage and attitudes changed in line with strategy
Effectiveness success rate	81% (+++)	70% (++)	44% (– –)	55%
Accountability success rate	74% (+)	69%	57%	70%

The most frequently used approach is to examine whether brand usage (and attitudes) changed in proportion to exposure to the campaign. There are three common ways to do this: by looking at variations over time, by looking at variations by region, or by looking at variations between individuals.

The most common approach is simply to look for correlations over time. For example, does the brand's performance tend to improve when the campaign is running? Does it tend to go into decline when the campaign stops? If there is a strong correlation between brand performance and communications activity, then it probably suggests that the campaign is working, and it may even be possible to estimate the size of the effect. A good example of this approach is the Honda case study (see below).

Honda

The 2004 Honda case study showed how website visits, call centre volumes and requested test drives surged during the integrated campaign and then fell away afterwards. For example, monthly call centre volumes:

Incremental profit was generated of at least £84m from a £47m campaign budget.

Source: Honda

It's easy to see why the correlation approach is so popular. Correlations between brand performance and campaign exposure are easy to understand, and often quite easy to find. But correlation is not the same as causation. Often there are other factors affecting brand performance that confuse the picture, causing 'spurious' correlations. For instance, seasonality is often a problem. Most markets are seasonal to some extent. For example, demand for hot foods tends to increase in winter; these products also tend to be advertised in the winter. As a result, sales and advertising nearly always correlate for hot foods, regardless of whether or not the ads work. Spurious correlations of this kind mean that simple comparisons between sales and marketing activity can often lead to quite misleading conclusions.

Similar problems arise with behavioural and attitudinal data. Just because awareness rises when the ads go on air, it doesn't necessarily mean that advertising is driving awareness – there could be something else going on. Because of problems like this, campaigns that rely on simple correlations between brand performance and exposure tend to be less accountable and less effective than those that use more sophisticated methods, as Table 46 shows (page 74).

Choosing a more appropriate measure of brand performance can sometimes improve things. Switching from sales to market share can make effects clearer, as was argued in Part 2, because it takes out the effects of market factors such as seasonality. Other methods, such as year-on-year comparisons, moving annual totals or rate of sale measures may also help.

However, regardless of which brand performance measure is chosen, other factors are usually still an issue. Market share may have risen, but how does one know that it wasn't due to price or distribution? At the very least, further analysis is usually necessary to discount such factors – showing that price and distribution remained static, for instance. And, ideally, one should account for such factors econometrically.

In fact, econometrics is usually just a more sophisticated version of the kind of analysis just discussed, in that it looks for correlations between brand performance and campaign exposure. The difference is that econometrics takes account of other factors as well. It is noticeable that many of the more successful IPA cases that use simple correlations to demonstrate effectiveness then go on to use econometrics to conclusively prove and measure the effect. Again, the Honda case study is a good example.

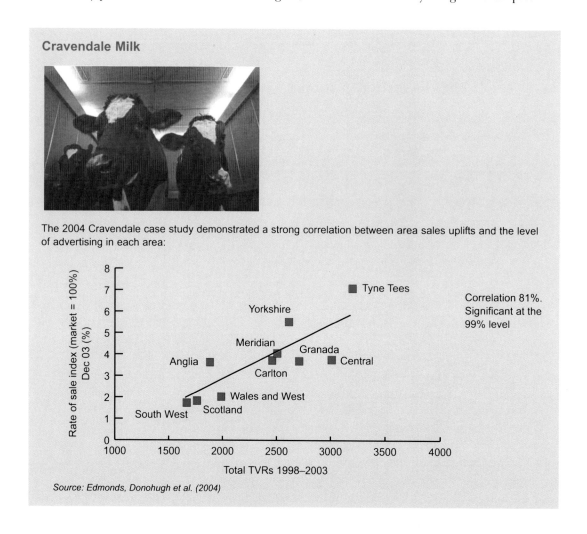

Cravendale Milk

The 2004 Cravendale case study demonstrated a strong correlation between area sales uplifts and the level of advertising in each area:

Source: Edmonds, Donohugh et al. (2004)

Marketing in the Era of Accountability

Another, less common, form of correlation analysis uses regional data. If there have been regional variations in media activity, then a simple correlation of brand performance with weight of exposure by region will sometimes show the effect of the campaign quite clearly.

Regional analysis of this kind is a good way to remove the effects of factors like price, product or packaging that are similar in all regions. The technique can also be used to extrapolate to the zero-exposure situation and hence estimate the overall impact of the campaign. An example of this approach can be seen in the 2004 Cravendale Milk case study (see opposite).

The Cravendale paper took regional analysis even further, by going down to the level of individual grocery stores to reveal the effects of different media. However, it should be noted that, once again, the paper used econometrics to provide the definitive measurements of effectiveness and profit returns.

The third kind of correlation analysis uses data on individuals. If true single-source data are available, it may be possible to show that individuals who were exposed to your campaign changed their behaviour in a way that others did not. This can be a powerful way to demonstrate advertising effectiveness. A recent example of this comes from the 2004 paper for More4 (see below).

More4

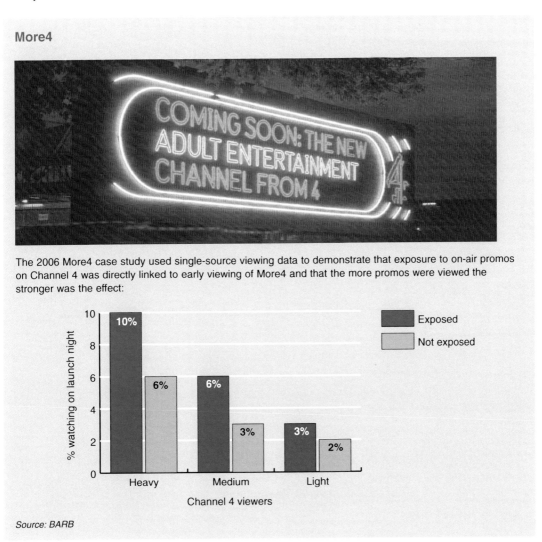

The 2006 More4 case study used single-source viewing data to demonstrate that exposure to on-air promos on Channel 4 was directly linked to early viewing of More4 and that the more promos were viewed the stronger was the effect:

Source: BARB

True single-source data record actual purchases and media consumption at the individual level. However, most marketers don't have access to such data. Tracking studies tend to record media recall, rather than exposure, and buying habits and intentions, rather than actual purchases. This leads to an extremely common mistake: the so-called 'Rosser Reeves Fallacy'.

The Rosser Reeves Fallacy

As long ago as 1961, Rosser Reeves wrote an influential book, *Reality in Advertising*, in which he observed that people who recalled advertising for a given brand were more likely to be users of that brand than people who did not recall the advertising. He proposed this as a proof of advertising effectiveness and as a means of gauging the level of effectiveness (by measuring the different levels of purchasing among recallers, 'the pulled', and non-recallers, 'the non-pulled'). In fact, we now know that generally people who already know and like a brand are more likely to recall communications about it. As a result, there is nearly always a correlation between campaign awareness and brand metrics at the individual level, but the correlation is not necessarily causal. The data usually show that people who recall your campaign tend to like and buy your brand. But that doesn't mean that your campaign works – it may well be that usage and attitudes are driving recall, rather than the other way around.

The frequency with which this mistake is made should not be underestimated. Nearly all IPA case study authors make it at some point, as do many research companies. But it is a mistake. **Simply showing that people who recall your campaign think well of your brand does not prove that it works**, and may be quite misleading. The Rosser Reeves Fallacy is another reason why campaigns that rely on simple correlations between brand metrics and media measures do badly in terms of accountability and effectiveness (see Table 49).

The Rosser Reeves Fallacy also illustrates another danger of the use of intermediate measures and objectives as an end in themselves. Intermediate measures of brand health will be powerfully influenced by the number of users of the brand as well as (perhaps) by successful marketing. So how can one be sure that the intermediate effects caused the business effects? As Feldwick (2002) points out, it can be 'impossible to distinguish cause and effect in such correlations', however sophisticated your analysis is. It is possible that in some situations intermediate measures of brand health are lagging indicators: they may not spur growth at all.

Another widely used approach to proving effectiveness is to demonstrate that brand usage and attitudes changed in line with the communications strategy, rather than exposure to the campaign or recall of it. Typically this means demonstrating an image shift that reflects the message of the campaign (see box opposite).

In general, this method provides fairly convincing evidence of effect (see Table 49, page 78). Certainly, this method is less susceptible to spurious correlations. For it to work well, market research should be closely tailored to the communications strategy: measure precisely those attitudes and behaviours that your campaign aims to change, not just a basket of standard, off-the-peg metrics.

Convincing as such proofs are, it is not usually possible to use this kind of analysis to quantify the business effect of the campaign, and it does not appear to promote effectiveness. This is again consistent with the earlier findings that intermediate KPIs are inferior to hard business ones and that focusing on narrow communications goals improves accountability, but not effectiveness (Part 2).

Proving that beliefs and attitudes changed in line with the campaign

Travelocity

The 2006 Travelocity case study demonstrated how using a well-travelled veteran TV travel presenter had improved its competitive image as an expert provider of inspiring travel:

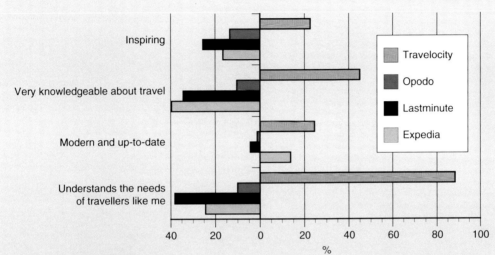

Source: Hall and Partners, Tracking

Tobacco Control

The 2004 Government Tobacco Control case study demonstrated how the campaign had raised awareness among smokers of featured diseases linked to smoking (but not of diseases that were not featured):

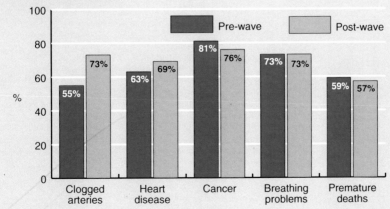

In general, **the most successful way to prove effectiveness without econometrics is to demonstrate that the user profile or product mix changed in line with the communications strategy** (see Table 49, page 78). For example, the campaign may have recruited a new consumer segment to the brand. Self-evidently this can be successful only if the strategy targeted such change. It will be quite a stretch to use this kind of analysis to quantify the business effect of the campaign, but it can provide powerful evidence of effect (i.e. it is good for accountability). Moreover, because as a metric it keeps minds focused on the strategy, it appears to promote effectiveness rather well. An example of this can be found in the 2006 Actimel case study (see below).

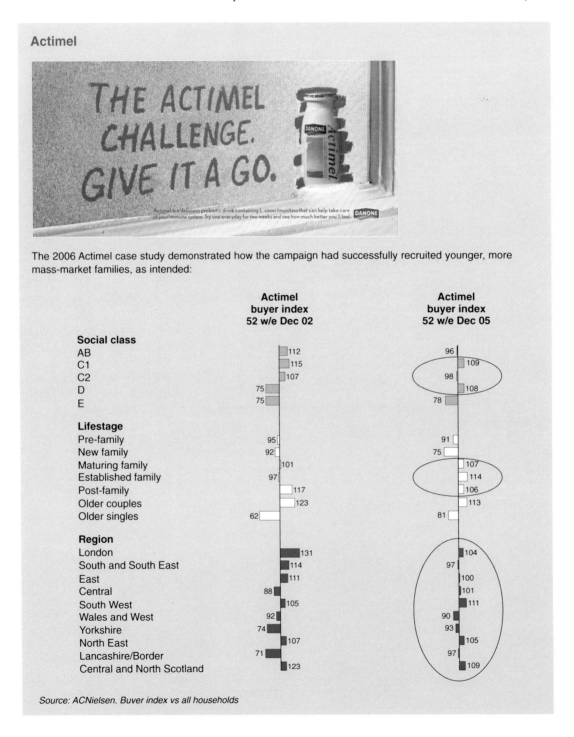

Actimel

The 2006 Actimel case study demonstrated how the campaign had successfully recruited younger, more mass-market families, as intended:

	Actimel buyer index 52 w/e Dec 02	Actimel buyer index 52 w/e Dec 05
Social class		
AB	112	96
C1	115	109
C2	107	98
D	75	108
E	75	78
Lifestage		
Pre-family	95	91
New family	92	75
Maturing family	101	107
Established family	97	114
Post-family	117	106
Older couples	123	113
Older singles	62	81
Region		
London	131	104
South and South East	114	97
East	111	100
Central	88	101
South West	105	111
Wales and West	92	90
Yorkshire	74	93
North East	107	105
Lancashire/Border	71	97
Central and North Scotland	123	109

Source: ACNielsen. Buyer index vs all households

Marketing in the Era of Accountability

Beware of area tests

So far, area tests (the comparison of 'silent' with 'exposed' areas) have not been discussed as an approach to testing and evaluation. They are often used as a simple way to measure the effectiveness of marketing activity. However, the dataBANK shows that **area tests are fairly unreliable as a means of promoting or demonstrating effectiveness** (see Table 50).

Table 50: Weakness of area tests

	Campaigns using area test data for sales, share or rate-of-sale	Campaigns using any data for sales, share or rate-of-sale
Effectiveness success rate	41% (−)	52%
Accountability success rate	34% (− −)	45%

This echoes a finding reported by Broadbent (1989) that, in a review of US area weight tests, only one in 20 produced conclusive results (Corkindale & Kennedy 1975).

The most common problem appears to be imperfect control areas. Even with a well-designed test, market conditions will vary from region to region for reasons that are outside the marketer's control. In some cases, the competition may even deliberately try to muddy the waters. Clients often compound these problems by using too few test regions and by not running tests for long enough.

Better data analysis can help make more reliable use of area tests. The regional correlation techniques described above can get more out of test data than a simple comparison of test regions versus controls. And econometric models that use regional data are even better. In fact, using such techniques may make formal regional tests somewhat redundant, since they can examine minor variations in weight and timing by region, without the need for silent regions.

This may be just as well. Silent regions, by their very nature, reduce the effectiveness of a campaign. Perhaps as a result, campaigns that use area tests are significantly less effective than those that don't, as Table 50 shows.

Use a balanced scorecard of business measures

Since Kaplan and Norton (1992) introduced the idea of the balanced scorecard as a framework for measuring the performance of companies, it has steadily gained momentum. The dataBANK suggests that a similar approach should be used for brands. With the exception of profit as a measure, it is not the case that any particular business effects reflect overall performance, but rather the *number* of them. As was shown in the Introduction (taking market share gain as the measure of overall performance, because it is most widely reported in the dataBANK), Table 51 reiterates that large share gains are associated with more numerous business effects in a highly significant (99% confidence) and strikingly proportionate relationship.

As will be shown later on, this correlation between the number of very large effects and share gain can be extended to soft intermediate effects, so the balanced scorecard approach is a more general recommendation. **There is a potential tension inherent between this scorecard approach and the general wisdom that focus promotes progress. The solution to this lies perhaps in focusing on the**

overall score, or 'metric of metrics', as this publication proposes. So long as the 'metric of metrics' wisely balances the individual measures according to their observed contribution to effectiveness, then there is little need to worry about the individual factors that constitute the score: just make sure the score keeps rising. The use of a 'metric of metrics' is discussed further later in this section.

Table 51: Large share gains are associated with more widespread business effects	
Number of very large business effects reported	**Market share gain* (average share points gain)**
0	3.4%
1	4.2%
2	9.9%
3	12.2%
4	11.0%
5	18.0%

*value share where available otherwise volume

Choice of business data

In Part 2, it was shown that market share was a much better KPI than sales. Focusing on market share rather than sales leads to better accountability and more effective campaigns. It therefore follows that **audit or panel data is better for evaluation than company sales data,** because they provide information on competitors and so allow market share to be measured. They are consequently more likely to promote effectiveness and accountability (Table 52).

Table 52: Potency of data types		Cases using audit or panel data	Cases using company sales data	Cases using direct-response data
Effectiveness success rate		55% (+)	52%	35% (– – –)
Accountability success rate		48% (++)	41%	44%

It was also shown in Part 2 that one of the more profitable ways in which marketing can work is by reducing price sensitivity, so allowing firms to charge higher prices. It is therefore important to take account of price effects when measuring the impact of marketing on your brand. **At the very least, this means focusing on value measures rather than volume. And, if possible, use econometrics to measure the price response explicitly.**

Table 52 also highlights the dangers of using simple direct-response data as a KPI. Because such data do not include a measure of profitability, or even share, they don't promote business effectiveness or even accountability (to more than a superficial degree).

Behavioural KPIs

If business measures are the primary metrics for evaluating most campaigns, then behavioural measures usually come next in the hierarchy. (A notable exception would be some non-profit campaigns, where behavioural change is the primary goal.) Clearly, behavioural KPIs should reflect detailed marketing objectives, and can be incredibly diverse. But a good rule is to **tailor your market research so that you measure precisely the behaviour you want to elicit**.

However, two important behavioural metrics for most clients (even some non-profit ones) are penetration and loyalty. It was shown in Part 2 that penetration should often be a key behavioural metric, with loyalty, if relevant, secondary.

Actual experience seems to reflect this. Among IPA cases, penetration is used to demonstrate effectiveness more than 10 times as frequently as is loyalty (see Figure 27). This is remarkable, given that most of these campaigns (as was shown in Part 2) claim to be targeting loyalty not penetration, but is no doubt a reflection of the relative intractability of loyalty.

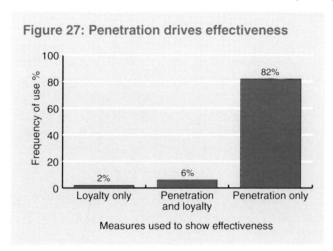

Figure 27: Penetration drives effectiveness

Loyalty is an unpopular metric for good reason. Figure 27 shows (as Ehrenberg has also shown) that **loyalty seldom increases except in tandem with penetration**. Furthermore, when loyalty does increase, **penetration gains are nearly always as big or bigger** (see Table 53).

Table 53: Penetration gains are usually larger than loyalty

	Relative scale of effects where both penetration and loyalty grow		
	Campaign affected penetration more than loyalty	Campaign affected penetration and loyalty equally	Campaign affected loyalty more than penetration
Frequency (% cases)	35%	50%	15%

This explains the earlier finding (of Part 2) that campaigns that target loyalty don't tend to be very effective, and that when they do work they mostly work by increasing penetration.

The corollary of this is that in the small number (8%) of cases when significant loyalty effects were recorded, they usually indicated a highly effective campaign that improved lots of different measures, including both penetration and loyalty. This does not make loyalty a particularly useful KPI – in practice it is just a very blunt way of measuring extremely large penetration effects – it is better to focus on penetration itself. At most, loyalty should be used as one metric among many in a balanced scorecard of behavioural measures.

Are campaigns strong or weak forces?

The data in this section, as well as those in Part 2, have already started to illuminate some of the battlegrounds of the long-running war between the 'strong' and 'weak' theories by testing Ehrenberg's observations on loyalty. But what of the broader picture?

The strong theory argues that marketing communications are a powerful force that can significantly manipulate consumer behaviour. In this theory, not only can marketing communications introduce new users to a brand, but they can also persuade new users to adopt it and thereafter increase repeat purchase behaviour, thus creating greater brand loyalty/share of category usage. In this theory consumers are either brand loyalists or promiscuous switchers, and communications can strongly influence the latter to adopt a different brand.

The weak theory argues that marketing communications exert only a weak influence on consumer behaviour – which is much more strongly influenced by experience of the brand. Consumers purchase from a repertoire of brands that they feel similarly good about (there is very little 100% loyalty in most categories). Repeat purchasing is more a function of product experience, pricing, distribution, competition and other external factors. Thus communications can significantly grow brands only by introducing new users to them, and from then on repeat purchasing follows rigid category patterns that cannot significantly be influenced by communications (apart from some gentle 'nudging' between repertoire brands). In this model brand loyalty does not differ greatly from one brand to another, with the partial exception that larger brands have slightly higher loyalty levels (as well as having more users – the so-called 'double jeopardy' effect). The only potent weak theory role for communications, apart from introducing new users, is to defend the brand against the recruitment of its users by competitors, by reminding them of its presence: reinforcement.

Proponents of each model (most famously John Philip Jones and Andrew Ehrenberg respectively) advance reams of data to support their points of view, while the instinctive support of many marketers lies with the strong theory. After all, who wants to believe that they cannot build loyalty and categories?

This publication has already demonstrated that **the building of loyalty is rarely a successful objective** for campaigns and, where it is achieved, it is usually only modest and accompanied by a larger growth in penetration. This is exactly what Ehrenberg would predict: loyalty to brands is essentially constant across a category (only varying slightly with share) and cannot be significantly influenced by marketing.

Ehrenberg also predicts another finding of the dataBANK (already shown) that to a large extent it matters little what the nature of the advertising message is (i.e. the communications strategy model being followed) – **what matters most is whether the advertising successfully raised the 'saliency' of the brand** (a widely misunderstood term that is discussed later). Clearly one cannot entirely decouple these two, since an important element of strategy development is the achievement of greater presence. But it does serve to focus the mind away from the minutiae of motivational analysis in strategy development and towards the more straightforward objective of reinforcing the presence and authority of the brand in the minds of its target consumers. **The fame model of advertising, which the dataBANK has shown to be the only significantly more effective one, is consistent with this Ehrenbergian view of the profitable role of advertising.**

If the strong theory prevailed, one would expect to see a lot of case studies demonstrating loyalty growth as the dominant effect of campaigns; in fact there is a conspicuous lack of examples of such campaigns in the dataBANK (as has been shown).

So **the dataBANK tends to side with the weak theory to some extent.** However, this publication has also shown that **following the weak theory too rigidly in the shape of espousing 'reinforcement' campaigns is a recipe for under-achievement. Marketing needs to focus on recruiting new users** (i.e. penetration growth) or 'filling the leaky bucket'; this is the commercially realistic facet of the weak theory.

Should campaign evaluation measure HAP or LAP?

The issue of what and how to measure when testing or evaluating communications is a live one, with a number of aggressively argued competing points of view. It is helpful to view the dataBANK findings in the context of these, and examine what light the data can shed upon them.

Most importantly, battle lines have been drawn between supporters of low-attention processing and supporters of high-attention processing – that is, between Heath's recent thinking about brand communications (Heath 2001) and the earlier approach of Millward Brown (to say nothing of the array of approaches that lie somewhere between these two models of thought). To some extent the weak theory accommodates these competing points of view as particular circumstances where narrower theories apply (rather like how Newtonian physics serves us well for low-speed motion but Relativity is needed to also explain observations at higher speeds). Thus it can be argued that the high-attention processing inherent within the Millward Brown model is a perfectly valid (if increasingly difficult to achieve) means of increasing brand saliency at the point of purchase decision making. As this part will evidence, **high-attention processing is not always necessary, and is not always sufficient**, but it is clearly still a feature of many effective campaigns.

Similarly the low-attention processing inherent within Heath's model is also entirely valid, since its modus operandi is to feed intuitive decision making through stored associations (engrams): 'Brand associations and their emotive links endure in memory beyond the point at which conscious recollection of the ad itself disappears' (Heath & Hyder 2005). The fact that these engrams are not necessarily accessible to conscious thought does not matter in the context of the weak theory – they have still served to raise the 'saliency' of the brand and hence prompted trial or reinforced existing usage patterns by the consumer. We just need a broader understanding of what saliency is; it is not only comprised of conscious brand awareness, consideration and brand associations, but also of the subconscious equivalents of these. Indeed there is an affinity between Heath's intuitive model of decision making and Ehrenberg's deterministic Dirichlet model of purchasing – both suggest at their core that human beings do not make such decisions in a very considered, rational way. Herd instinct more like.

Perhaps, therefore, it is indicative that Heath's elegant tests of his theory on campaigns for Butchers dog food and Standard Life (Heath & Hyder 2005) were both conducted among non-users of the brands, measuring the advertising power to generate trial, not influence loyalty.

There is some support in the dataBANK for Heath's model of marketing effect. In particular, the data seem to support his assertion that the creation of conscious brand awareness and imagery is not always necessary for strong business effects. **In fact, about a third of cases describing effective campaigns reported little or no effect on brand awareness** (see Figure 28).

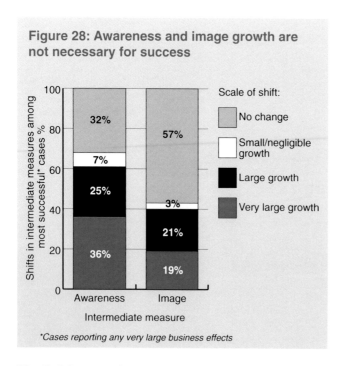

Figure 28: Awareness and image growth are not necessary for success

Cases reporting any very large business effects

The link between brand image and effectiveness seems to be even more tenuous. **Over half of all campaigns that proved to be highly effective in business terms reported little or no improvement in brand image**. This is consistent with the finding of Part 2 that brand image is one of the hardest things to change, and that campaigns that attempt to do so don't tend to be terribly successful.

It is also consistent with the weak theory, since that theory argues that evaluative brand imagery (that which measures consumers' views of the fitness for purpose of the brand) is actually a function of market share. Ehrenberg argues that users of all brands in a category tend to evaluate them identically; only the differing number of users of each brand creates apparent image differences.

None of this means that brand awareness and image are unimportant, or that low-involvement processing is better than high-involvement processing. In this the data are consistent with the findings of Ipsos-ASI (Mundell *et al* 2006): 'Even though we can clearly see that LAP can have a significant impact on brand choice, there is nothing to suggest that having low HAP and high LAP is preferable.' Figures 29 and 30 show that *very large* **improvements in brand awareness and image do seem to be good predictors of business success**; 80% of campaigns reporting very large awareness gains also produced very large business effects, which is significantly above average.

However, *more modest* **gains in awareness and image do not seem to be particularly good predictors of success**. In fact, campaigns reporting no gains in awareness and image do about as well as those reporting large ones.

It is a common assumption that conscious brand awareness is a necessary condition for business success. These data suggest that it is not. While very big improvements in brand awareness and image are usually a sign of success, there are plenty of campaigns that are highly effective in business terms without any such improvements at all. Improvements in awareness and image are not a necessary condition for effectiveness. Later on, it will be shown that they are not a sufficient condition either (though this is implicit within the data above).

Marketing in the Era of Accountability

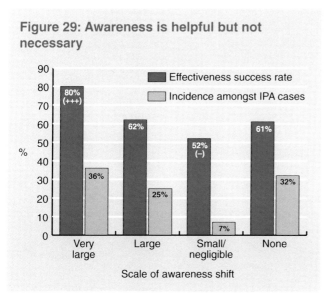

Figure 29: Awareness is helpful but not necessary

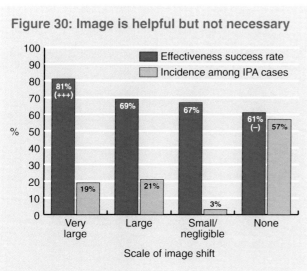

Figure 30: Image is helpful but not necessary

Similarly, it is commonly assumed that campaigns must stand out in order to be effective. Heath has argued against this and the dataBANK supports his views. Table 54 shows that **campaigns that demonstrate standout (through measures such as advertising awareness and recall) do not perform any better than those that don't.**

Clearly the majority of effective campaigns do demonstrate standout, so the data are not advocating the abandonment of standout as an objective (nor does Heath for that matter). But the data show that standout is not necessary, and to the extent that demonstrating standout does not appear to improve the chances that the campaign will be effective, nor is it generally sufficient (see Table 54). The implications of this for research and evaluation are clearly considerable and so the issue is explored further later in this section.

Heath goes further, suggesting that conscious awareness of marketing communications can be unhelpful for smaller brands that lack any functional advantage, because it encourages disadvantageous

Table 54: Campaign standout does not drive effectiveness or accountability

	Campaigns that demonstrated standout	Campaigns that did not demonstrate standout
Incidence among all cases	79%	21%
Effectiveness success rate	59%	59%
Accountability success rate	67%	69%

comparative rational consideration with stronger brands. Again, this view is consistent with the weak theory, since such consideration inevitably evokes and involves competitors and might therefore tend to undermine the saliency built for the brand. However, the dataBANK does not really seem to support this conclusion. Even for small brands, there is not much difference in effectiveness between campaigns that demonstrate standout and those that don't (see Table 55).

Table 55: Campaign standout does not drive effectiveness for small/niche brands

	Campaigns that demonstrated standout	Campaigns that did not demonstrate standout
Incidence among all small/niche brand cases	79%	21%
Effectiveness success rate	75%	74%
Accountability success rate	79%	70%

The data already reported (in Part 4) certainly also support Heath's general assertion that long-term effects are promoted by emotional messaging, because such messages are more durably recorded in the brain (and therefore result in more durable 'saliency'). Emotional strategies therefore tend to be more efficient than rational ones. The fact that emotional strategies can work powerfully even in rational categories (categories where rational consideration plays a powerful role in brand evaluation) suggests, however, that the power of emotional messaging lies not so much in its persuasiveness as in its memorability (conscious or subconscious). Indeed, Heath has suggested that the most powerful advertising is able to engage high-attention processing (usually with 'news') for short-term effect, as well as low-attention processing (usually with emotional engagement) for more durable long-term effect; this has long been a conspicuous property of Gold and Grand Prix prize-winning cases at the IPA Effectiveness Awards.

A corollary of Heath's suggestion that rational messaging tends to disadvantage brands without functional advantages can be found in the relatively greater importance of rational strategies to successful leader brands. Leader brands are usually the brands best able to support a stream of innovation, and so benefit from saliency generated by rational comparison with other brands and high-attention processing. This is especially the case in 'high-think' categories where saliency is more likely to be fuelled by rational messaging.

So Heath's theory would advise caution in relying on intermediate effects (and in particular on individual effects that assume a single mode of effect) in the measurement of effectiveness. The dataBANK very strongly supports this conclusion.

Brand awareness and image shifts are unreliable predictors of effectiveness

Of the four types of measure used to demonstrate campaigns' effects on consumers, awareness and image were conspicuously less associated with effectiveness (Table 56). Perhaps because of this, they were also less good for demonstrating accountability.

Table 56: Potency of measures used to demonstrate consumer effects

	Cases that used brand awareness	Cases that used brand image	Cases that used brand consideration	Cases that used blind vs branded product tests
Effectiveness success rate	46% (– –)	48%	74% (+++)	75% (+)
Accountability success rate	45%	44% (–)	71% (+++)	75% (+)

In contrast, **brand consideration is a more reliable indicator of effectiveness because it is more closely linked to actual behaviour. Branded vs blind product tests are also a very good measure** (although rarely used) and appear to provide a much more reliable gauge of the strength of the brand than image scores do.

Looking specifically at the relationship between brand awareness and profit growth further illustrates the unreliability of brand awareness (see Table 57).

Table 57: Brand awareness is an unreliable indicator of success

	Cases reporting very large increases in brand awareness	Cases reporting any very large intermediate effects
% reporting very large profit increases	30% (–)	37%

By now the reader will not be surprised that, despite these findings, awareness and image massively dominate the measurement of marketing impact on consumers (in 82% and 66% of cases respectively, compared to just 19% using brand consideration measures): common practice is far from best practice.

Use a balanced scorecard of intermediate measures

As with business measures, the data suggest that no single intermediate measure is particularly good at predicting business success. In part this is because different campaigns work in different ways and no one measure will work in all situations, but that alone cannot explain the striking uniformity of the relationship (Table 58). It is also due to the complexity of brands as they exist in the minds of consumers. The reason the term 'brand health' is preferred here (to 'brand equity') is because it reminds us that, like the health of a person, the health of a brand is multi-dimensional, and cannot

Table 58: Potency of intermediate measures

Cases reporting very large effects on	Direct effects	Differentiation	Image	Awareness	Quality	Commitment	Fame	Trust
Effectiveness success rate	82%	81%	81%	80%	79%	78%	77%	68% (–)
Accountability success rate	74%	68%	65%	76% (+)	62%	69%	64%	64%

easily be summed up by any single number. One would not expect a single measure of human health (e.g. blood pressure) to reliably predict overall health. Similarly, no single measure of brand health is likely to reliably predict the consequent business health of the brand. Feldwick (2002) provides a more detailed and extremely useful discussion of the complexities of the issue.

The link between brand trust and effectiveness is particularly weak (which corroborates the finding in Part 2, that aiming to build trust is a weak strategy), but to a great extent they are all much of a muchness. They are clearly very blunt measures in the context of effectiveness. So the value of these measures is to indicate *how* a campaign is working, not *whether* it is working.

However, **the number of intermediate effects does turn out to be a very reliable predictor of business success** (though sadly it is not yet recognised as an accountable measure), see Table 59.

Table 59: Number of very large intermediate effects reported

	0	1	2	3+
Effectiveness success rate	46% (– – –)	68%	75% (+)	88% (+++)
Accountability success rate	68%	77%	77%	68%

Clearly, very effective campaigns have a wide range of effects, and so any single measure may understate the likely effects. **The more measures that move, the better.**

This observation is proof of the wisdom of the late Simon Broadbent's observation that the art of evaluation is like 'spotlights on a statue from different angles': the more you use, the more clearly you can see what you are looking at. Again the analogy with human health is helpful: health insurers increasingly assess their risk using a basket of health measures. Brands should do the same.

But what of the unwelcome complexities introduced by the monitoring of numerous intermediate effects, with perhaps differing levels of influence over business success? This argues for the practice by research companies, suggested earlier in this section, of using aggregated 'metric of metrics' to monitor brands and test communications material. This provides a single *compound* metric to focus on rather than a *single* measure of just one factor (some companies already do this).

But the use of multiple intermediate measures as a measure of brand health has another important advantage, especially if the 'metric of metrics' is refined as a predictive tool over time using modelling. Monitoring a broader base of measures reduces the problems arising if any of them turn out not to be leading indicators after all. Perhaps this too explains why multiple intermediate effects are a more reliable indicator of business success than single ones.

The finding that multiple intermediate metrics can form the basis of a more reliable leading indicator of brand performance also begins to explain why some communications strategies appear more effective than others. It was shown in Part 2 (Table 19) that some objectives produce more intermediate effects than others, and that some are more effective in business terms than others (Table 20). These data are reprised below in Table 60.

Table 60: The factors for business success of campaign objectives

| Campaign objective | The factors | | Level of business success |
	Average number of very large intermediate effects generated	Success rate vs the objective	Effectiveness success rate
Fame	2.3	37%	78% (++)
Trust	2.2	12%	72%
Differentiation	2.0	35%	70%
Quality	2.0	28%	73%
Commitment	1.9	26%	70%
Direct behaviour	1.8	46%	67%
Awareness	1.8	45%	67%
Image	1.7	27%	68%

The table shows that **some objectives are easier to achieve** than others, while **some have broader effects** than others. It also shows that these two factors seem to explain a lot of the differences in business effectiveness that were observed in Part 2.

For instance, Part 2 concluded that **strategies that aim to improve commitment and trust tend to be relatively ineffective**. The table shows why: these are the most difficult measures to improve.

Similarly, Part 2 concluded that **campaigns that focus on brand awareness or direct responses are highly accountable, but not particularly effective**. Now one can see why. These campaigns have a good track record of achieving the objective, but have quite narrow effects. The target measure improves, but not much else happens. This is good for accountability – the effect of the campaign is fairly clear – but it's bad for effectiveness. Really effective campaigns tend to shift lots of intermediate measures.

Also, Part 2 concluded that **improving quality perceptions is a more effective strategy than merely aiming to build a strong brand image**. And again one can see why: this is a more easily attainable goal, and tends to have wider effects.

And finally, one can see why fame is such a successful strategy. **Brand fame is relatively easy to achieve and has the widest effects of all**. This also illustrates the qualitative difference between fame and awareness (or standout). Fame builds a *broad* sense of brand health by creating perceptions that a brand is widely valued, whereas awareness merely creates knowledge of its presence. The latter is often insufficient for effectiveness.

Beware of single measures of advertising standout

If multiple measures are good for predicting effectiveness, then it follows that single measures are less reliable. This is especially true of advertising standout, whose unreliability as a predictor has already been demonstrated. Standout merits closer inspection for three reasons:

1. It is the single most common measure of advertising impact.
2. It is the fastest-growing measure used in case studies: it was used in 24% of cases in the period 1980–1996 vs 63% of cases in the period 1998–2006.
3. Many marketers have developed go/no-go standards based on a single predictive KPI of advertising standout.

The dataBANK shows that marketers should not rely on advertising standout as a single measure. Table 54 (page 92) showed that **campaigns that demonstrate standout do not seem to be any more effective than those that don't**. Standout may be important, depending on the strategic model being used (e.g. rational news-based advertising relying on high-attention processing for the majority of its effect), but it is not a reliable indicator of effectiveness in general. What is more, the reliability of standout as an indicator of effectiveness when used as a single measure is even weaker than in general use (see Table 61).

Table 61: The reliability of campaign standout as a single indicator of business success		
	All campaigns demonstrating standout	**Campaigns only demonstrating standout**
Effectiveness success rate	59%	40%

The 2006 Tropicana case study illustrates the potential dangers of relying on standout alone to measure the effectiveness of a campaign. Tropicana's 'New York' campaign performed poorly in terms of the Awareness Index (the Millward Brown proprietary measure of the power to standout), yet proved to be highly effective in terms of sales and profit (see opposite).

This was further explored in an analysis conducted by ACNielsen and reported in the 2006 Tropicana case study. ACNielsen examined more than 20 brands where both an Awareness Index (AI) had been calculated and where the power of the campaign to generate volume sales growth had been measured econometrically. They failed to find a statistically significant correlation between 'standout power' and 'sales power' (see Figure 31).

Tropicana's experience of the Awareness Index

The Tropicana TV campaign achieved an Awareness Index of only 3, well below the UK norm of 6. Yet the advertising alone drove an 11% volume growth for the brand and reduced price elasticity by 40%. A positive profit return was reported. The success of the campaign was attributed to its power to engage low-attention processing and thus bypass the cognitive mental processes evaluated by the Awareness Index

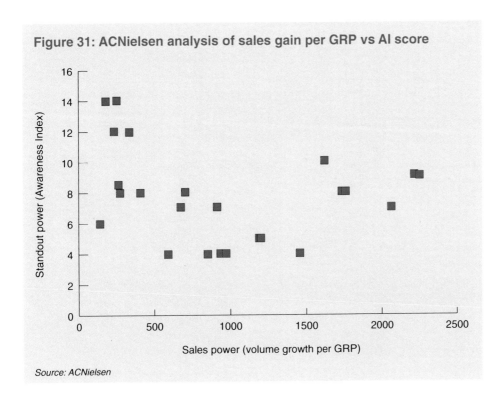

Figure 31: ACNielsen analysis of sales gain per GRP vs AI score

Source: ACNielsen

Likeability is a better measure (as single measures go)

The dataBANK reveals that, even if standout has a role, then at the very least, marketers should broaden their range of measures to include advertising mode-relevant response measures such as likeability, communication or persuasion. All of these response measures demonstrate a greater link to profit generation and business effects in general than standout, especially likeability (see Table 62).

Table 62: Reliability of response measures as indicators of success

	Cases demonstrating likeability	Cases demonstrating persuasion	Cases demonstrating communication	Cases demonstrating standout
% reporting very large profit increases	36% (++)	31%	28%	24%
Effectiveness success rate	72% (+)	67%	67%	59% (−)

Standout has been shown to be a particularly poor predictor of effectiveness when used on its own. But it should be noted that none of these measures is infallible and best practice is to look for a balanced scorecard of multiple effects.

The finding that **likeability is a better predictor of business results than standout** is consistent with the theory of low-involvement processing. It should also be noted that **likeability seems to be a better predictor than persuasion**. In Part 4, it was argued that persuasion is a primarily rational communication mode, so this finding seems to be consistent with the idea that emotional communications are more effective than rational ones.

The importance of likeability is also corroborated by a number of other research studies, most notably the 1991 American Advertising Research Foundation (ARF) copy research project (Haley & Baldinger

1991), that have shown that **likeability of advertising is the best predictor of sales effectiveness**. The same study, more fully analysed by Eagleson and Rossiter (1994), showed that 26 out of the 35 pre-testing measures examined performed so poorly that they could safely be rejected – and of the nine that were worthwhile, around half measured advertising likeability in some form or another.

Beware of pre-testing

Clearly, pre-testing and post-evaluation measures 'travel together', since the former is largely intended to be a predictor of the latter. So all that has been said about intermediate measures applies equally to pre-testing. If a pre-testing methodology is intended to predict a single response measure such as standout, and that measure is a poor predictor of business success, then the pre-testing methodology is likely to be flawed.

However, an even greater uncertainty is introduced with pre-testing: the level and nature of consumer exposure is removed from the reality of the in-market experience. This may limit the ability of pre-testing to predict even the chosen response measure, let alone true business success.

Most of the cases in the dataBANK (73%) use some form of pre-testing data to demonstrate effectiveness. It seems fair to assume that case studies that included pre-testing results would have achieved good results – or why use them? On this assumption, if pre-testing really did lead to more effective campaigns, then one would expect these cases to show bigger effects than those that did not use pre-testing as part of their evidence. One might also expect them to win more awards. In fact the reverse is true. **Cases that reported favourable pre-testing results actually did significantly worse than those that did not** (see Table 63).

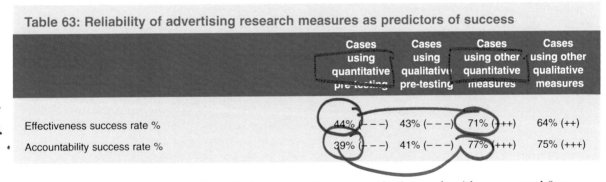

Table 63: Reliability of advertising research measures as predictors of success

	Cases using quantitative pre-testing	Cases using qualitative pre-testing	Cases using other quantitative measures	Cases using other qualitative measures
Effectiveness success rate %	44% (– – –)	43% (– – –)	71% (+++)	64% (++)
Accountability success rate %	39% (– – –)	41% (– – –)	77% (+++)	75% (+++)

Moreover, the same was as true of qualitative pre-testing as quantitative, and neither was good for accountability. The data are clearly not suggesting that pre-testing is entirely worthless, but do cast considerable doubt on the ability of such research to reliably pick winners.

This is consistent with Heath's model, which argues that because many of the impressions of brands held in consumers' minds have been stored using low-attention processing of communications, people cannot reliably answer questions designed to elicit the impact of campaigns on brands. They are not consciously aware of all the messages that have been stored, even when they are triggered at the moment of brand choice.

Some collateral measures are worth monitoring

The dataBANK also records what collateral measures were reported by case studies (effects not targeted by the campaign but believed to be indicative of its effectiveness). A number of these effects are not in fact associated with business effectiveness in general – for example, media coverage of the campaign, easier staff recruitment and retention, greater staff satisfaction and increased staff productivity. However, three collateral effects are worth noting because they are associated with business effects and accountability (see Table 64).

Table 64: Reliability of collateral effects as measures of success

	Cases reporting improved investor awareness	Cases reporting improved investor ratings and share price	Cases reporting improved supplier relations
Effectiveness success rate	88% (+++)	81% (+++)	70% (++)
Accountability success rate	79% (+)	74% (++)	69%

Given the very close association of these collateral effects with business measures, notably profitability, it is perhaps not surprising that they prove to be good indicators of business success.

Summary: golden rules for measurement

1. Use a balanced scorecard of multiple measures to evaluate your campaign, rather than a single metric. It is the number of measures that improve significantly that indicate commercial success, not any single movement.

2. If you do want a single KPI to focus on, use a 'metric of metrics'.

3. Evaluation measures should reflect campaign objectives and strategy. Don't just rely on standard, off-the-peg measures. Tailor your research to reflect the precise way you expect your campaign to work.

4. Some metrics are more important than others. Hard business measures come first, behavioural measures come second, intermediate measures come third.

5. Use hard data to measure the effectiveness of your campaign. Use intermediate measures to explain how it works and (with many combined as a metric of metrics) as provisional leading indicators of effectiveness, until hard results become available.

6. The primary objective of all commercial campaigns is profit, so if possible use econometrics to measure financial payback.

7. More generally, use a balanced scorecard of business metrics to measure commercial performance. Pay attention to the number of different business effects, not just one single measure.

8. Include measures such as the share price, investors' ratings, etc. in your scorecard. These reflect an overall judgment of the business's long-term value.

9. Try to account for other factors when judging the business success of your campaign. Focus on market share rather than sales. Use value measures rather than volume. If possible, use econometrics to take full account of all the factors that affect demand.

10. Make sure your data sources include information on the competition. Always look at how you perform relative to them, so as to take account of factors that affect the whole market. Beware of sources (such as company sales data, web traffic, direct response rates) that don't account for market factors.

11. Look for correlations between campaign effects and *exposure* to the campaign, not recall of it. In particular, showing that attitudes to a brand correlate positively with recall of its advertising does not prove that the advertising works (the 'Rosser Reeves Fallacy').

12. Area tests are not a panacea. They are hard to do well, and are often inconclusive. Choose test regions with care, and run the test for a decent length of time. Remember, silent regions lose you sales.

13. Analyse your regional data carefully. Don't just compare test regions vs controls – look for detailed regional correlations between performance and weight. If possible use econometrics. It may even be possible to measure effectiveness using 'natural' regional variations, without the need for a formal test.

14. Penetration is generally a more important metric than loyalty. But ideally, use a balanced scorecard of behavioural metrics that reflects how communication might be expected to work for your brand.

15. Attitudinal measures are useful, but don't rely on them as your primary measure of effectiveness. You may not be measuring the key attitudes. They may not even be measurable.

16. If you are using attitudes to measure effectiveness, use a balanced scorecard, rather than focusing on a single metric. Commercially effective campaigns move *many* intermediate measures not just one. Movement of a single intermediate metric is a highly unreliable indicator of success.

17. In particular, beware of just using direct response rates or awareness shifts to evaluate your campaign. Campaigns that focus on these metrics tend to hit their KPIs, but have narrow effects and under-perform in business terms.

18. Improvements in brand awareness and image are neither necessary nor sufficient to produce business success. Campaigns can work in other ways. Use a balanced scorecard of brand diagnostics, paying more attention to measures like consideration and branded-vs-blind preference.

18. Improvements in brand awareness and image are neither necessary nor sufficient to produce business success. Campaigns can work in other ways. Use a balanced scorecard of brand diagnostics, paying more attention to measures such as consideration and branded-vs-blind preference.

19. Similarly, standout is neither necessary nor sufficient for an effective campaign. Use a balanced scorecard of impact measures, paying particular attention to emotional responses such as liking.

20. Interpret pre-test results with caution. Most pre-testing methodologies are intended to predict some attitudinal measure, which may or may not be related to business success. Even if the test predicts attitudes correctly, it may not predict effectiveness.

21. Rigorously evaluate any pre-test predictions and other leading indicators against actual subsequent business results. Use the findings to refine your basket of 'balanced scorecard' metrics.

7 Payback and remuneration

The calculation of payback is a fraught but vital area of evaluation. Indeed (in the case of for-profit firms at least) one can argue that **payback is the ultimate measure of effectiveness**.

It is widely argued that expenditure on communications should be thought of as a kind of investment. When a factory owner invests in a new piece of machinery, his production capacity increases, and the result (hopefully) is a stream of extra profits over subsequent months and years. Similarly, when a marketer invests in a piece of communication, demand for his products increases, and the result should be a similar stream of additional profits. Accountants know how to measure the return from the first kind of investment, but precisely how should the payback from marketing be measured and reported? Until that question is answered, marketing cannot assume its rightful place alongside other forms of responsible investment.

This part will examine the use, misuse and drawbacks of the most commonly quoted payback measure, 'ROI'. It will also examine some of the factors that drive profit returns. Finally, this section will pull together a number of the strands of learning emerging from the dataBANK, in the shape of design recommendations for value-based remuneration schemes for marketing teams and their agencies.

The use, abuse and drawbacks of ROI

The term 'ROI' (return on investment) is widely used to describe various measures of the effectiveness and efficiency of marketing. It has become popular because it makes marketing and communications seem accountable and financially sound. However, the use of the term tends to be very loose, meaning different things in different contexts, as Ambler (2004) has pointed out.

Use

In fact, return on investment is an accounting concept with a well-defined meaning. It is simply the ratio of the profits generated by an investment to the amount of money invested. So, for marketing, the appropriate ROI measure is:

$$ROI = (profits\ resulting\ from\ marketing) \div (marketing\ spend) \times 100\%$$

For commercial firms, ROI can really only be calculated in one way (see box overleaf). To do otherwise completely undermines the accountability of marketers and their agencies, and should never happen.

Abuse

The dataBANK reveals many shortcomings in the measurement of payback in actual practice. Relatively few IPA cases measure financial payback properly (as was shown in the Introduction), and it's safe to assume that things are even worse in the day-to-day world of marketing outside the competition. One or more of the following mistakes are often made.

1. Failing to calculate payback at all

Even when not-for-profit cases are excluded, not all cases attempt to measure financial payback. And many use only non-financial measures to demonstrate effectiveness. Some compound this error by using financial terms like 'ROI' to refer to non-financial measures such as direct-response rates or awareness shifts. This unfortunately makes the marketing and communications community look ill-informed at best, and perhaps even dishonest.

2. *Miscalculating the incremental sales effect*

When calculating return on marketing expenditure (ROME), it is very important to **focus on the truly *incremental* returns from marketing activity**. One needs to be very clear on the difference between the 'base case' (without the effect) and the 'investment case' (with the effect). Frequently, the short-term contribution of communications is overestimated. Two mistakes are particularly common.

The first is to assume that all sales growth was due to the campaign. In fact, **other factors may have played a role, and should be accounted for**, ideally using econometrics or some test-and-control technique.

The second mistake is to count all direct sales as effects of direct response communications. This tends to overestimate the contribution of those direct channels. In fact, many direct sales are not incremental sales at all, but would have been made anyway, with or without the campaign. And those that are incremental are probably the combined result of a number of different channels, not just direct activity.

On the other hand, long-term effects are often under-estimated. As was suggested in Part 3, for most brands a large proportion of share of voice is devoted to maintaining market share from year to year. In particular, **marketing for mature brands is often about *defending* sales, not increasing them**. To calculate profit returns properly in such cases, it is necessary to estimate the long-term decline in sales that would occur if marketing support were withdrawn.

3. *Treating revenue as profit*

Many IPA cases base their payback calculations on additional sales revenue generated, as Binet (2005) and Sharp (2007) have reported. But **additional revenue is not equal to additional profit**. There are very few businesses where additional sales incur no costs of supply at all – the additional costs associated with those sales must also be taken into account, otherwise payback will be massively overestimated. This is an elementary error, yet analysis of the dataBANK suggests that roughly two-thirds of cases make it, as a result of which most payback calculations are totally flawed.

4. Using the wrong profit margin

When calculating ROME, it is important to use the correct profit margin. **The profit margin on incremental sales is often much higher than the average profit margin.** This is because, when sales increase by relatively small amounts, the extra volume can usually be pushed through the supply chain with no increase in fixed costs. This means that the appropriate profit margin to use for ROME is the brand's rate of marginal contribution, not the 'fully loaded' net profit (which includes fixed costs). This is an important distinction, as rates of net profitability are typically between 5% and 20%, whereas rates of marginal contribution can be anything from 40% up to 100% (the latter in the case of 'zero marginal cost' businesses like airlines and telecoms). The implication is that a lot of marketing pays back more quickly than a cursory glance at the client's profits might suggest.

Drawbacks

ROI in the shape of ROME is a measure of the financial efficiency of a campaign. It is a potentially useful ratio because it allows you to compare the payback from different activities even if they have had different budget levels in the past. Given the choice between two campaigns or media, one would be well advised to go for the one with the higher ROME.

But, although ROI can be a useful measure of the efficiency of marketing in some circumstances, as Ambler (2004) has pointed out, **ROME is not a ratio that firms should try to *maximise*.** Rather, they should be trying to maximise the absolute payback from marketing. Ambler's reasoning was reviewed in Part 2. In particular, problems arise when ROME is used for budget setting (rather than budget allocation). As Ambler points out, the best way to boost ROME in the short term is often to cut marketing expenditure, even though this may reduce the firm's total profits and destroy shareholder value. The use of ROME as a KPI for budget setting is thus extremely dangerous.

Ambler's preferred alternative is to set profit targets in absolute (money) terms and to measure payback as the difference between incremental profit and the cost of marketing (rather than the ratio). This is in fact a very important distinction and forms the basis of the recommended approach to payback that follows.

Calculating payback in the longer term

So far, ROME has been discussed only in the context of short-term sales and profit increases. The challenge for practitioners is that most advertising investments are true 'investments' in the sense that costs are being incurred now in pursuit of some longer-term benefit. In fact it's probable that most 'brand-building' communications do not demonstrate profitable payback on the basis of immediate, short-term sales uplift. With encouragement from the IPA, clients and agencies are now beginning to make some progress in the measurement of long-term effects. However, the calculation of payback from long-term effects requires some additional mathematics, which have until now been largely ignored in this part.

Accountants have a very clearly defined method for calculating the payback from longer-term investments, known as 'discounted cash flow' analysis (DCF). DCF underpins a lot of contemporary management thinking on shareholder value management. So, anyone who seriously believes that marketing expenditure is an investment and not a cost, should **use the DCF method to calculate financial payback**, if they are looking at anything other than short-term effects.

In essence, DCF allows an investor to look at a single number that assesses the value of an investment in terms of whether the aggregate stream of future profits exceeds the cost of the investment. Because money in the future is worth less than money now, estimates of future profits need to be discounted at some suitable interest rate. The resultant number is called the 'net present value' (NPV) of the project. Strictly speaking, only investments demonstrating the likelihood of a positive NPV should be undertaken. Without going into the mathematical details, the steps involved are as shown in the accompanying box.

The calculation of net present value (NPV)

Step 1: Estimate the stream of extra profits generated by the communications, both while the campaign is running and in the months and years afterwards (in the same way as for ROME).

Step 2: Take account of how *quickly* the campaign pays back. Some campaigns deliver short-term results, others take years to pay back. Use DCF to calculate the 'present value' (PV) of the stream of extra profits generated by the campaign.

Step 3: Finally, subtract the cost of the campaign* from PV to calculate the NPV. If the NPV is positive, then the campaign creates value for shareholders, and must be judged to be successful. If the NPV is negative, then value has been destroyed, and the campaign must be judged a commercial failure.

If the campaign is a recurring expense stretching into the future, then the cost of the campaign needs also to be projected and discounted in order to compute a 'present value' (i.e. cost) that can be subtracted from the benefits to yield the NPV.

The DCF approach to calculating payback is very closely related to the idea of brand valuation. Most brand valuation methodologies (e.g. the Interbrand methodology) attempt to estimate the incremental profits resulting from the use of a particular brand name. The brand valuation is then simply the NPV of those incremental profits. One may therefore view the DCF approach as an attempt to calculate the contribution of marketing to the financial value of the brand. As such this measure is aligned to growth in the 'intangible' value of the brand – increasingly a key area of interest to analysts and investors (IPA 2006).

Confusingly, as was observed in Part 2, some people use the term 'brand equity' to refer to the long-term financial value created by brands and marketing. This is particularly unhelpful in the light of the other meanings of the term outlined by Feldwick (2002), and will not be used here to describe NPV.

NPV is arguably a much better KPI to focus on than short-term ROME. First, it takes account of both long- and short-term effects. Second, focusing on NPV should ensure that all marketing activity is aligned with the interests of shareholders, whereas (as discussed above) focusing on ROME can sometimes lead to shareholder value being destroyed.

As with short-term ROME, the DCF approach to calculating payback is not easy. The difficulty comes in Step 1, estimating the stream of extra profits generated. Accurate measurements usually require econometrics, or at the very least some sort of test-and-control approach. But such measurements can only be complete long after the event, when the campaign has finished making its mark. So unless the effects of the campaign are completely short term, earlier calculation of NPV will require the projection of those effects onward as well as of market dynamics. This involves an element of judgment. Although managers face exactly the same problem when estimating the payback from more conventional investments like new factories, the calculation will be 'highly conjectural', as Ambler puts it.

It should be noted that because brand valuation too is based on DCF, it is also 'highly conjectural'. Estimates of the financial value of a brand are highly dependent on assumptions about future cash flows. This is why valuations sometimes change quite dramatically over time, and why the same brand may be worth more to one owner than another, as Feldwick (2002) points out.

Nevertheless, the DCF approach is the only way of calculating financial payback that stands up to proper financial scrutiny and takes account of both long- and short-term effects properly. **The DCF approach should therefore be the gold standard for measuring effectiveness** for commercial communications. Until now, very few IPA cases have attempted a proper DCF analysis of payback. As the measurement of longer-term effects becomes more commonplace, this must change.

Factors affecting payback

Although the disclosure of properly measured payback is rare among IPA case studies, examination of the 39 cases that do provide accurate ROI figures reveals a wide spectrum of degrees of payback. The data in Table 65 are 'returns on marketing expenditure', since this is how profit growth is usually reported, rather than NPV. They therefore express incremental profit as a percentage of expenditure. Fortunately we need not be concerned here with Ambler's observations about the dangers of such measures in general, since all the cases also demonstrated positive momentum for the brands. So there is no question of ROI being 'artificially' generated at the expense of brand momentum by cutting investment.

Table 65: Incidence of reported levels of ROME (as 'ROI')

ROME range (%)	Number of cases	% of total
≤50	10	26%
50–100	3	8%
100–200	9	23%
200–400	8	21%
400–600	4	10%
600–800	2	5%
≥800	3	8%
Total	**39**	**100%**

Of course, these campaigns are likely to be more profitable than average (the average ROME for these 39 cases is 595%, that is to say they pay back almost six times over), however, the table does show what sort of return can be achieved when marketing works well. But what circumstances make a campaign more or less profitable? The dataBANK can shed some light on this issue.

In Part 3, it was shown that growth in market share seems, all other things being equal, to be proportional to excess share of voice. If this is true, then it follows mathematically (see Appendix) that ROME is highly influenced by three factors that relate more to the category than to the campaign itself.

The first factor affecting ROME is the profit margin on incremental sales. **Firms that make big margins will tend to have high ROME.** This is why pricing strategy is so important. Anything that allows a firm to charge higher prices is likely to be very profitable, because all the benefits fall straight to the bottom line. Not only that, increasing price often also increases the returns from *other* forms of marketing. In fact, a quite modest increase in price can dramatically increase the payback from marketing communications, as Sharp (2007) has argued. Conversely, heavy discounting through trade promotions may reduce margins to the point where other forms of marketing are completely unprofitable.

The evidence from the dataBANK suggests that the use of marketing to support higher pricing (i.e. reduce price sensitivity) is linked to success in increasing profits, and that this is easier in more emotional categories (see Table 66).

Table 66: The power of supporting pricing in emotional categories

	Nature of consumer decision making in category		
	Predominantly emotional	Equally emotional/rational	Predominantly rational
% cases reporting very large effects on price sensitivity	6%	5%	0%
% cases reporting very large effects on profit	29%	26%	16%

The second factor affecting ROME also concerns profit margins, but is more subtle. Because it is determined by the rate of marginal contribution on incremental sales, **ROME is likely to be higher for firms that have high fixed costs but low marginal costs,** such as airlines.

The third factor affecting ROME is the degree of competition. As Dyson (2003) has pointed out, ROME is proportional to the value of the market, and this is one of the biggest factors affecting payback. But the IPA dataBANK also suggests that ROME is inversely proportional to competitive spend, and big, valuable markets tend to have high levels of spend. These two effects tend to cancel one another out. The dataBANK suggests that what matters is the average advertising-to-sales (A/S) ratio for the category. **A high A/S ratio for the category implies a low ROME.** In this way, communications can act as a barrier to entry into a market, as was the case with the Optrex campaign (Part 3).

Aside from these three factors, ROME will be determined by the responsiveness of the brand to communications. Are there any consistent patterns in this? The dataBANK can answer this question in two ways. The first is to use share of voice analysis, as was done in Part 3. The second is, once again, to look at the incidence of very large business effects. The two approaches (the first two rows of data in Table 67) tell a fairly consistent story.

First, **small brands tend to be more responsive to marketing** than big ones. Small brands are usually less well known than big ones, so there is more news to tell. (The dataBANK shows that awareness gains are more common for launches and small brands.) There is also more scope for increasing penetration and gaining market share.

Second, **brands in newer categories tend to be more responsive** than those in older, more mature

Table 67: How return varies by brand and category

	Brand size		Category life stage		Category growth	
	Small/ niche	Larger	Newer	Mature	High/medium growth	Low growth/ declining
Share points gained per 10% excess SOV	1.3	0.3	3.3	1.2	1.9	1.2
Effectiveness success rate	73%	66%	78%	66%	75%	69%
% cases reporting very large penetration increases	34%	20%	40%	22%	34%	30%

categories. Again, such products tend to be more newsworthy, and there is often scope for increasing category usage as well as market share, so penetration gains tend to be particularly big.

Third, **brands tend to be more responsive to marketing when the market is buoyant**, and less responsive when it is depressed. This might seem to suggest that marketers should cut their budgets when times get tough, as they often do. However, if your competitors are cutting their budgets, the cost of buying share of voice will fall, and this will tend to *increase* your ROME. Maintaining spend when a category is in the doldrums is hard to do, but there is evidence from Biel & King (1999) and others (e.g. Hillier 1999) that those who manage it outperform the competition in the long run.

A corollary of the above findings is that **the effects of marketing tend to be more dramatic in the earlier phases of a brand's life**. (As was discussed in Part 3, the effects of marketing tend to be particularly big for launches, although it is difficult to disentangle the specific contribution of communications in such cases.) As a brand matures, growth rates tend to slow down, and the role of marketing tends to shift from short-term growth to long-term maintenance. As discussed above, **this does not mean that marketing for mature brands is unprofitable**, it just means that financial payback needs to be calculated in a different way, with more emphasis on the long-term and *maintenance.*

Implications for the design of payment by results schemes

The design of a reliable value-based remuneration scheme (otherwise known as payment by results) will almost certainly require the use of leading indicators as well as lagging indicators. Leading (intermediate) indicators can provide a prompt basis for provisional remuneration so that the cashflow of agencies does not suffer unduly. But, as this report has demonstrated, this will not form an entirely reliable basis, even when multiple leading indicators are used. So final adjustments to remuneration should follow the availability of the balanced scorecard of lagging (hard) indicators at the end of the reporting period.

Clearly, **realistic targets for both leading and lagging indicators should be set in advance**. However, these targets will need to measure the contribution of the communications to progress, not simply the level of progress. If the wind is against the brand then progress will tend to be slow, whereas if there is a following wind, progress on some metrics may come easily (as has just been identified). 'Smart targets' should take account of this.

Leading indicators

A balanced scorecard of leading indicators should be drawn from as *many* of the following brand health metrics as are available and relevant to the brand (in order of likely importance).

- Behavioural consumer metrics, such as claimed trial or usage and perhaps loyalty. Include any direct sales results, but do not use these as the only measure of behaviour. If new usage occasions or new user segments are targeted, then these should also be measured.
- Attitudinal consumer metrics, especially those measuring brand consideration and the fame (or authority) of the brand, measures of perceived relative quality and differentiation (not necessarily functional – perceptual emotional differentiation is at least as important). If relevant, include measures of awareness and brand image, but choose the latter wisely: they should have a proven influence on choice of brand.

It is recommended that a model be developed that reflects the relative importance of these leading indicators to explaining subsequent lagging business indicators. The model can be used to define a single metric of metrics to simplify the remuneration decision. This model should be developed and refined on an annual basis by an independent third party, to improve its predictive capability. Always remember that it is unlikely that any single brand health measure will prove a reliable leading indicator.

Lagging indicators

Again, **a balanced scorecard of brand business metrics** is recommended as the lagging indicator of success. Ideally, econometric modelling should be used to isolate the contribution of any one element to the overall business success of the brand, and to quantify the effects of external factors.

As discussed above, the scorecard should always include some measure of financial payback; it is important that this is calculated correctly, and that long-term effects are taken into account as well as short-term ones. Beware of focusing solely on ROI (which only measures efficiency); look at the absolute payback in terms of NPV (which measures effectiveness).

Clearly payback measures are likely to be the most important element of the scorecard, but other hard metrics should be included as appropriate to ensure broad progress is being made. As many of the following metrics as are available and relevant to the brand should be included:

- the profit contribution of the communications
- its impact on price sensitivity (from reliable audit data)
- contribution to market share growth/maintenance
- actual consumer penetration from robust panel data (and, if relevant, loyalty data too).

In each case some kind of modelling will be needed to determine what the baseline would have been without the communications activity – most likely a decline in the majority of key metrics. Again a single metric of metrics that encapsulates this balanced scorecard is recommended.

It is also important that movements in these metrics are related to the scale of investment made in the communications – that some measure of efficiency is included as well as whether scorecard targets were met. With profit, this is clearly achieved through ROME, but for market share growth this will require relating growth to SOV–SOM norms for the category. This approach could be extended to other hard metrics to take account of whether SOV was sub-equilibrium or not.

Summary: golden rules for payback and remuneration

1. Payment by results schemes should include both leading indicators (based on intermediate data) and lagging indicators (based on hard business results).

2. For both lagging and leading indicators, use a balanced scorecard of several different measures.

3. Summarise the results of each scorecard with an overall 'metric of metrics', based on a weighted average of the individual scores.

4. For commercial firms, always include an assessment of financial payback.

5. Make sure that payback is correctly calculated, based on the incremental profit generated by the campaign (compared with what would have happened if it hadn't run). Remember to take account of other factors that affect sales besides the campaign.

6. Don't confuse revenue with profit and make sure that the correct profit margin is used!

7. Include any price effects in your calculation, as this is often where the biggest payback comes from.

8. Take account of both long- and short-term effects, using DCF.

9. Use NPV to measure the effectiveness of your campaign in financial terms.

10. ROI in the form of ROME is a useful measure of financial efficiency, but beware of using it as a KPI. Aiming to maximise ROME can lead to budget cuts and lower profits.

11. When assessing the overall performance of a campaign against targets, bear in mind the scale of the task. Expect stronger growth from young brands, in younger, more buoyant or less competitive markets. For more mature brands and those in tougher markets, merely maintaining demand may be an achievement.

8 Conclusions and implications for further research

A recurring theme throughout this publication is the tension between *effectiveness* (doing the right thing) and *accountability* (being seen to do the right thing). In the post-Enron era, accountability has become a hot topic in all areas of business, including marketing, and quite rightly so. Measuring the effects of marketing is an important first step towards making it work better.

But **what is important, and what is easy to measure, are not always the same thing**. This publication has argued that a narrow view of accountability often distorts marketing priorities, leading to waste and inefficiency. In particular, it has been argued that **focusing on a small number of intermediate measures, such as awareness levels or direct response rates, can reduce effectiveness and profitability**.

In order to be both effective and accountable, marketers need to measure all the right things. It has been argued in this publication that this means taking a broader view of the many ways marketing can work, both short term and long term. And also that it means adopting a **'balanced scorecard'** approach to evaluation, based on an appropriately weighted mix of business, behavioural and intermediate data. If single measures of success or failure are required, then a **'metric of metrics'** is preferable to a single tracking score or pre-test result. Econometrics can be a particularly valuable element in this data mix, since it measures the impact of marketing in hard business terms.

Aside from the issue of effectiveness and accountability, this publication has hopefully demonstrated the potential of the IPA dataBANK as a business tool. It is hoped that the recommendations made throughout will be used not only to help improve the day-to-day practices of marketing, but also to spur much needed improvements in the measurement of effects. Clearly applying the general principles advocated in this publication to the requirements of a particular brand requires further work. This is certainly the case in improving value-based remuneration schemes. Hopefully those who have benefited from these findings will publish their own case studies and so stimulate a virtuous circle of improvement.

As the number of cases continues to grow, the complexity and robustness of analyses that the data can support will also grow. Future mining of the data will hopefully go deeper than it has been possible to go here, and maybe illuminate some of the more controversial findings.

References

Ambler, T. (1999) 'Where does the cash flow from?' Editorial, *Journal of Marketing Management*, **15**, 9–10, (8 November).

Ambler, T. (2004) 'ROI is dead, now bury it', *Admap*, (September), Issue 453, pp. 43-45.

Armstrong, J. & Green, K. C. (2007) 'Competitor-oriented objectives: the myth of market share', *International Journal of Business*, **12**, 1.

Baker, C. (ed.) (1993) *Advertising Works 7*, NTC Publications, Henley-on-Thames, UK.

Barwise, P. (1999) 'Advertising for long-term shareholder value', *Admap*, (October), Issue 399, pp. 40–42.

Biel, A. & King, S. (1999) 'Advertising during a recession', in *Advertising In a Recession* (edited by P. Barwise) pp. 21–28, NTC Publications, Henley-on-Thames, UK.

Broadbent, S. (1989) *The Advertising Budget*, NTC Publications for the Institute of Practitioners in Advertising, Henley-on-Thames, UK.

Buck, S. (2001) *Advertising and the Long-term Success of the Premium Brand*, World Advertising Research Center for the Advertising Association, Henley-on-Thames, UK.

Buzzell, D. & Gale, B. (1987) *The PIMS Principles*, The Free Press, New York, USA.

Cook, L. & Holmes, M. (2004) *Econometrics Explained*, (edited by L. Binet) IPA, UK. Available as a download from: www.ipa.co.uk/documents/Econometrics.pdf

Corkindale, D. & Kennedy, S. (1975) *Measuring the Effects of Advertising*, pp. 100–125, Saxon House/ Lexington Books, Lanham, USA.

Dyson, P. (2003) 'Advertising profitability: size matters', *Admap*, (November), Issue 444, pp. 41–43.

Eagleson, G. & Rossiter, J. (1994) 'Conclusions from the ARF's Copy Research Validity Project', *Journal of Advertising Research*, (May/June), **34**, 3.

Ehrenberg, A. (2000) 'Repetitive advertising and the consumer', *Journal of Advertising Research* (Dec/Jan), **40**, 6.

Ehrenberg, A. (2005) 'My research in marketing', *Admap*, (May), Issue 461, pp. 46–49.

Feldwick, P. (2002) *What is Brand Equity, Anyway?* World Advertising Research Center, Henley-on-Thames, UK.

Feldwick, P. & Heath, R. (2007) '50 years using the wrong model of TV advertising', MRS Conference paper, Brighton, UK, (March).

Green, L. (ed.) (2007) *Advertising Works 13*, World Advertising Research Center, Henley-on-Thames, UK.

Haley, R. & Baldinger, A. (1991), 'The ARF Copy Research Validity Project', *Journal of Advertising Research*, (April/May), **31**, 3.

Heath, R. (2001) *The Hidden Power of Advertising*, Admap Publications, Henley-on-Thames, UK.

Heath, R. & Hyder, P. (2005) 'Measuring the hidden power of emotive advertising', *International Journal of Market Research*, **47**, 5, pp. 467–486.

Hillier, T. (1999) 'Successful Competitive Strategies for Recession and Recovery: Evidence from PIMS', in *Advertising In a Recession* (edited by P. Barwise) pp. 43–51, NTC Publications, Henley-on Thames, UK.

Hoad, A. (ed.) (2004) *Advertising Works 13*, World Advertising Research Center, Henley-on-Thames, UK.

Hollis, N. (1994) 'The link between TV ad awareness and sales. New evidence from sales response modelling', *Journal of the Market Research Society*, **36**, 1.

IPA (2005) *Evaluation*, joint industry best practice guide, IPA, ISBA, MCCA & PRCA, (August), London, UK.

IPA (2006) *The Intangible Revolution*, IPA, (November), London, UK .

Jones, J. P. (1990) 'Ad spending: maintaining market share', *Harvard Business Review*, **68**, 1, (January/February).

Kaplan, R. & Norton, D. (1992) 'The balanced scorecard: measures that drive performance', *Harvard Business Review*, **70**, 1, (January/February).

Kendall, N. (ed.) (1999) *Advertising Works 10*, NTC Publications, Henley-on-Thames, UK.

McKinsey & Co (2000) *The Power of Loyalty*, White paper published online (authors Cigliano, J., Georgiardis, M., Pleasance, D. & Whalley, S.).

The Marketing Society and McKinsey & Co. (2004) *The Coming of Age of Marketing*, The Marketing Society, London, UK.

Morgan, A. (1999) *Eating the Big Fish*, Wiley, New York, USA.

Mundell, J., Hallward, J. & Walker, D. (2006), 'High-attention processing: the real power of advertising', *Admap*, (July/August), Issue 474, pp. 40–42.

Peckham, J. (1974) 'Marketing advertising patterns', Proceedings of ESOMAR Congress, Hamburg, Germany.

Prue, T. (1998) 'An all-embracing theory of how advertising works', *Admap*, (February), Issue 381, pp. 18–23.

Sharp, A. (2007) 'Demonstrating payback', in *Advertising Works 15* (Edited by Green, L.) World Advertising Research Center, Henley-on-Thames, UK.

Tellis, G. (2007) 'Advertising Effectiveness in Capitalist Markets', Presentation to WARC Measuring Advertising Performance Conference, February 2007, WARC.com.

Twose, D. (2005) *Driving Top-line Growth*, IPA dataMINE No. 1, World Advertising Research Center, Henley-on-Thames, UK.

Appendix

Further details of all the analysis summarised in this publication can be found in a technical appendix, available as a downloadable pdf file.

To access the Appendix go to www.warc.com/datamine2, with a copy of this publication in front of you.

About the authors

Les Binet
European Director, DDB Matrix

Having read Physics at Oxford, Les took an M. Phil. in Artificial Intelligence at Edinburgh University. His research there focused on the use of computer models to study the way human beings process language. In 1987, he joined the Account Planning Department at BMP (now DDB London), where he turned his modelling skills to the problem of measuring the effects of advertising. He currently heads DDB Matrix, DDB's in-house econometrics consultancy.

Over the years, Les has worked for a wide range of clients, including Unilever, Heinz, Nestlé, Volkswagen, Johnson & Johnson, Kraft, Sony, AXA, and Anheuser Busch. He has also played an important part in establishing DDB's reputation for effectiveness, having won more IPA Effectiveness Awards than anyone else in the history of the competition. Since 2001, he has served on the IPA's Value of Advertising Group, helping to promote effectiveness and evaluation in the wider marketing community. In 2004 he was elected an Honorary Fellow of the IPA, in recognition of his services to the advertising industry, and in 2005 he was Convenor of Judges for the IPA Effectiveness Awards. Les helped to design and launch the new version of the IPA dataBANK, and is actively involved in promoting its use as a tool for research.

les.binet@ddblondon.com

Peter Field
Marketing Consultant

Having graduated from Cambridge, Peter Field spent 15 years as an account planner in advertising, working at DDB and AMV•BBDO, before going on to manage the planning departments of Bates and Grey. For the last 10 years he has pursued a consultancy role supporting both clients and their agencies, as well as starting a training partnership (Express Train) for the advertising and marketing industries, and supporting Eatbigfish, (the challenger brand consultancy) in its early years. Over the last 25 years he has worked in most categories and on over 90 brands.

Peter was a member of the IPA Value of Advertising Group for five years, and set up the IPA dataBANK and ran it in its early years. He was a judge for the IPA Effectiveness Awards in 1998. His educational activities currently include module editor for the IPA Excellence Diploma. He has spoken at many educational events, including those of the IPA, ISBA, *Admap*, *Marketing Week* and The Marketing Forum. In 1999 he contributed a chapter to *Advertising Works 10* on early learning from the dataBANK and more recently has contributed a chapter to the *Handbook of Advertising* (to be published by Sage this year) that draws heavily on data from the dataBANK. In 2006 he was elected an Honorary Fellow of the IPA.

peter.field@dsl.pipex.com

The IPA dataBANK

The IPA Effectiveness dataBANK represents the most rigorous and comprehensive examination of marketing communications working in the marketplace, in the world. Over the 26 years of the IPA Effectiveness Awards competition, the IPA has collected over 1000 examples of best practice in advertising development and results across a wide spectrum of marketing sectors and expenditures. Each example contains up to 4000 words of text and is illustrated in full by market, research, sales and profit data.

Purchasing IPA case studies

Member agencies are allowed a maximum number of 25 free case studies in any given calendar year, after which they will be charged at £17 each. Alternatively, members can sign up to www.WARC.com at a beneficial IPA rate and can then download case studies as part of that subscription.

Further information

For further information, please contact:

Information Centre
Institute of Practitioners in Advertising
44 Belgrave Square
London
SWIX 8QS

Telephone: +44 (0)20 7235 7020
Email: info@ipa.co.uk
Website: www.ipa.co.uk.

About www.WARC.com

The cases contained in the IPA dataBANK can also be accessed through WARC.com, the largest single source of intelligence for the marketing, advertising, media and research communities worldwide. WARC.com spans over 45,000 articles, case studies, research papers, news reports and summaries, augmented with best practice papers, practical guides, daily news, email bulletins and statistical data. Its collection of case histories features all the IPA cases since 1980, together with case histories from similar award schemes around the world, including the USA, Canada and Australia.

WARC.com supplies its users with information in key areas critical to their success, including communications effectiveness, marketing and brand strategy, media planning and buying, market research and methods, and consumer insight and behaviour. This business-driving resource is used by advertising and media agencies, blue-chip advertisers and marketers, research companies, media owners, marketing consultants and top business schools.

Index

econometric modelling
    measuring profit 24, 77–78
    use of 27–28, 77, 80
economies of scale
    brand size and advertising spend 47–49, 108
    emotional campaigns 63–64
Ehrenberg, Andrew 31–32, 88, 90
    emotional involvement campaigns 55, 56
    brand size influencing effectiveness 63–64
    effectiveness 57–65
    market conditions effecting 62–63
    mature and declining categories 63
    premium brands 62
    TV advertising 69–70
    versus rational campaigns 61–62, 92
fame campaigns 36–38, 55
    brand size influencing effectiveness 63–64
    effectiveness 57–58, 61, 96
    TV advertising 70
Feldwick, Paul 20, 70, 82, 94, 107
Felix's TV advertising 73
Gale, B. 13
government information campaigns
    attitude KPIs 34
    information campaigns 56
Green, K. C. 25
Haley, R. 99
Heath, R. 34, 64, 70, 89, 91–92
high-attention processing (HAP)
    versus low attention processing 89–93
Hillier, T. 109
Hollis, N. 98
Holmes, M. 77
Honda 79, 80
humour in advertising, effectiveness of 65–66
Hyder, P. 89
image
    brand 37–38, 89–93
individuals
    analysing advertising effectiveness on 81–82
information campaigns 55–56, 64–65
IPA (Institute of Practitioners in Advertising)
    case studies 5, 9, 11–12, 120–121
    dataBANK 5, 11–18, 120
    Effectiveness Awards 5, 9, 11
Jones, John Philip 41–42, 47–49, 88
Kaplan, R. 85
Kennedy, S. 85
key performance indicator (KPI)
    attitude shifts 34
    behavioural 87–88
    market share 24–26, 86